Beyond
Political
Correctness:

Are There Limits to This Lunacy?

by
David Thibodaux, Ph.D.

HUNTINGTON HOUSE PUBLISHERS

Huntington House Publishers
P.O. Box 53788
Lafayette, Louisiana 70505

Library of Congress Card Catalog Number 94-76352
ISBN 1-56384-066-9

---◇---

Contents

Chapter Six

Chapter Seven

Chapter Eight

Chapter One

———————————— ◇ ————————————

Political Correctness:
Beyond Sensitivity

This is my second book on the so-called politically correct phenomenon. I was originally compelled to deal with this subject at length by my deep concern over the effects this movement has had and is continuing to have on education in this country as well as the broader sociopolitical impacts on the culture at large. It has been and continues to be my position that the politically correct movement (and all its attendant "isms" such as multiculturalism, Afrocentrism, radical feminism/genderism, environmentalism, deconstructionism/poststructuralism, etc.) has turned the educational system of this country into a system of indoctrination where civil debate, open inquiry, logical analysis, and even historical and scientific fact have been sacrificed on the altar of a political and social agenda and all the politically correct notions upon which that agenda is based. The politically correct hegemony has been and is being enforced with intellectually dishonest tactics ranging from vicious personal attacks on those who take issue with any item on the PC agenda (*ad hominem* reasoning articulated with epithets like racist, sexist, homophobic, Eurocentric, insensitive, etc.) to distortions of fact (evidenced by the ongoing revision of history) which border on lies. Even more disturbing is that hiring and firing of faculty as well as the granting of tenure and promotion have been highly politicized by this movement on campuses across the country.

This movement has had its crosshairs trained on the very heart of American culture and the traditions (the Judeo-Christian tradition, the work ethic, the traditional family, etc.) upon which that culture was founded. Some of the advocates of politically correct ideas have been honest enough to admit that their ultimate goal is to "deconstruct" everything from notions of what constitutes "great" literature to "masculine and feminine character structures" upon which sexual identity and gender roles are based. I began my first book on this subject by citing the following examples of the kinds of ideas being pushed by the PC crowd.

- A man and a woman having a candlelight dinner is "prostitution."
- The list of "great literature" was put together by "high-Anglican a— to underwrite their social class."
- Any piece of writing "has so many different meanings that it has no meaning at all."
- History is what is important to you.
- The Constitution of the United States of America is "the embodiment of the White Male with Property Model."
- The "real" Son of God was black and was born four thousand years before Jesus.

For those who think it couldn't possibly get any more weird, here are some new politically correct "ideas" I have come across.

- "Conventional heterosexuality [is] absurd."
- Pedophilia is "not intrinsically wrong."
- Mark Twain was gay, or at least bisexual.

- Huckleberry Finn was black.
- The fact that the tassels on graduates' mortarboards (the caps worn at graduation ceremonies) are black is "a racial issue."
- It is not possible for blacks to be racists.
- The subject of da Vinci's *Mona Lisa* was "a battered woman," and her compelling and mysterious smile "is typical of people who have lost their front teeth."

Given these new "developments," perhaps it is clear why I find myself compelled to weigh in on this subject again. Just when I thought it couldn't possibly get any worse, it just keeps on getting weirder and weirder.

My first book on this subject, *Political Correctness: The Cloning of the American Mind*, has been out for over a year and a half, and mine is not the only book to deal with this subject. But, in spite of the books and cartoon strips and media programs and articles on the topic of PC, I still find myself being asked in interviews that I have done and continue to do across the United States and in Canada to define the term *political correctness*. I believe there are two reasons that many people still cannot say exactly what PC is. First of all, the term has been so widely used (perhaps *overused* would be the more appropriate word) that its specific meaning has become blurred. Secondly, because the term PC has become laughable, the bonafide disciples of PC have begun using other terms to describe themselves and their agendas (such as Multiculturalism and Outcome-Based Education) further confusing the discussions, which I have found to be a typical tactic of the PC crowd.

Most people are familiar with the politically correct movement as it relates to language. Basically, one is not supposed to use language that is in any way "offensive." Now, that might sound simple and even noble, but it gets tricky. As I pointed out in my first book, if one really listens to what is going on today, one is left with the very clear impression that there are only certain groups who enjoy constitutional protection from being offended. Those groups include, of course, some womyn [PC *sic*] (like

Anita Hill and Hillary Rodham Clinton) but not all womyn
(like Phyllis Schlafly and Nancy Reagan), certain ethnic
groups (like Hispanics and Latins) but not all ethnic groups
(like Irish and Cajuns), certain racial groups (like Negroes
and American Indians) but not all racial groups (like
Asians and Jews), and certain sexual "orientations" (like
gays and lesbians) but not all sexual orientations (like
heterosexuals). The status of bisexuals as a group that
enjoys "constitutional protection from being offended"
remains unclear. In fact, bisexuals really have it hard.
They may be the only group left that *everyone* agrees is all
messed up (see chapter 4, "The Gay Nineties"). I'm sure
we'll have a march soon to correct that.

Let me admit that one of the positive effects of the
whole politically correct movement has been to remind
us of the power of words to hurt. No decent, thinking
human being desires to inflict pain on others, even inadvertently. But, as is always the case, there comes a point
at which even good ideas pushed too far cross the deli-
cate line between the sublime and the ridiculous. Clearly,
academia has pole vaulted across that line, and we increasingly find our attention drawn to nonsense and di-
verted from the real issues of our time. This also diverts
attention from the truly insidious aspects of the politically
correct movement and the real agendas, many of which
have already been accomplished.

The March 1992 issue of *Measure*, an academic newsletter, defines political correctness as

> the process of structuring the faculty and student
> body to reflect percentages of females, minorities,
> etc., in the general population, and to alter a cur-
> riculum to exaggerate positives or eliminate or de-
> emphasize negatives about certain individuals or
> groups of people.

While this is true, I do not think this definition goes
far enough. The PC movement has politicized the entire
educational system of this country, not just our universities, and this politicization has as its major agenda to
"deconstruct" Western civilization generally and Euro-

pean/American culture specifically by attacking it as "racist, sexist, homophobic, and oppressive." Anything that
can even remotely be considered "traditional" is a target,
from traditional values to the Judeo-Christian tradition to
the work ethic to the traditional family to the Constitution of the United States. "Deconstructing" the texts produced by this culture to unearth racism, sexism, and
homophobia is the new national pastime of many academics.

Still, with all the attention that has been called to this
issue in the media and all the clear evidence that the PC
agenda is already being implemented, in fact, in many
ways has already been implemented, there are, amazingly,
still those who deny that there even is such a thing as PC.
As one might suspect, many if not most of those doing
the denying are, for the most part, academics who talk
and act strangely like PC stereotypes.

In the summer of 1991, Barbara Bergmann, the president of the American Association of University Professors (AAUP), appointed an ad hoc committee to discuss
and formulate a public position on the political correctness question. This committee issued a statement on 30
July 1991. This statement, "identified by General Secretary Ernst Benjamin as a statement from the Association,
was released to the national press. The Statement was
printed in the Fall 1991 *Footnotes*, where it is identified as
an AAUP statement." In this "Statement," "critics of 'political correctness' are described as 'self-righteous,' and
their arguments characterized as 'sloganeering, name-call-
ing.' " The "Statement" goes on to accuse those who dare
to speak out against PC, of "irresponsible use of 'anecdotes' and by being motivated by an 'only partly-con-
cealed animosity toward equal opportunity and its first
effects of modestly increasing the participation of women
and racial and cultural minorities on campus' " (*Measure*,
March 1992, No. 104, pp. 1–2).

This charge, that those of us in the professoriate who
have challenged the PC movement and expressed concern over where it is leading us, base our arguments on
"anecdotal evidence," is one that I have heard repeatedly.

The apologists for the PC movement, which has become institutionalized in our educational system, suggest that professors like myself use stories of outrageous events to stir people up when, they imply, these "anecdotes" are either made up or exaggerated, isolated occurrences.

Now, the PC apologists are correct in suggesting that the use of anecdotal evidence can violate logical argument. In other words, using a single, strange story that occurred on one campus to suggest that a major movement is underway in education across the country would be illogical. But, it is equally illogical to suggest that we should simply dismiss with a shrug the hundreds of "anecdotes" that have appeared and continue to appear on an all but daily basis in media outlets from the *Chronicle of Higher Education* to the major networks' evening news broadcasts, which clearly indicate a disturbing pattern.

In an article published in *Measure*, No. 104, March 1992, John M. Ellis refers to the AAUP's "Statement" that charges critics of PC with the "irresponsible use of anecdotes" and maintains that

> the authors' [of the "Statement"] own arguments are conspicuously vague and unsupported: we are never even told which critics or which incidents they have in mind. Are they referring to the Stanford core course controversy, to the events which led to the cancellation of Professor Stephan Thernstrom's course at Harvard, to the attempt at Duke to exclude National Association of Scholars members from important faculty committees, to the disruption of Vincent Sarich's anthropology class at Berkeley, or to the unconstitutional restrictions on freedom of speech in codes such as those adopted by the University of Michigan and the University of Wisconsin?

Ellis goes on to point out that the authors of the AAUP "Statement" do not even explain what they mean by "political correctness." He asks,

> Does it refer narrowly only to overt public confrontations involving issues of free speech and

inquiry? Or does it instead refer more broadly to the associated phenomena of the politicization of the curriculum and reading lists, the attack on the western canon as sexist and racist, or the resegregation of faculties and student bodies, all of which are occurring all across the country?

Mr. Ellis concludes by asserting,

> It is simply not credible to claim that developments which have become highly visible at Harvard, Stanford, Berkeley, Duke, Michigan, Smith, San Francisco State, UCLA, Wisconsin, CUNY, Texas, and Bennington, to mention only these, are not affecting "lots of American campuses." (p. 3)

Perhaps one of the most prominent academics denying the existence of a politically correct movement is Catharine Stimpson of Rutgers University. According to *U.S. News & World Report*, at the 1993 meeting of the Modern Language Association (a PC bastion), Professor Stimpson called those of us who have spoken and continue to speak of this phenomenon "fatheads" and "compared political correctness to UFO's." At this same meeting where the existence of political correctness was being denied by Ms. Stimpson, papers were being presented with titles such as "Jane Austen and the Masturbating Three-Button Jacket," "Between the Body and the Flesh: Performing Lesbian Sadomasochism," "The Poetics of Ouija," and "Transvestite Biography." In one session, Sara Suleri of Yale claimed that a donation to the university to set up a chair in Western civilization should be called "a chair for colonialism, slavery, empire, and poverty," while in another session, Steven Wartofsky of Loyola University of Chicago spoke about "a desire to forget history . . . [which] will begin at next year's MLA ... with the displacement of white male Eur-Americans' texts" (*U.S. News & World Report*, 18 January 1993, p. 25).

Now a rational person might be tempted to ask how in the name of logic could anyone attending such a meeting (referred to appropriately in the *U.S. News* story as "the 'Gong Show' of the academic world") maintain that

PC does not exist and is not, in fact, alive and well, one might even say thriving, on our campuses today? Carl Raschke, professor of religious studies at the University of Denver, provided one possible answer when he pointed out, "The American intelligentsia has a tremendous capacity for what psychologists call 'denial'" (*The Chronicle of Higher Education*, 9 January 1992, p. A-3). Then again, one might be inclined to give my PC colleagues, who are, after all, intelligent, articulate, well-educated people, the benefit of the doubt and say they are *not* simply in a state of denial, but that would lead to the troubling suspicion that they know exactly what they are doing, at which point the PC movement ceases to be amusing. Personally, I stopped laughing some time ago. Perhaps, the following quotations from my colleagues in the professoriate across the country will offer some insight as to why.

As I pointed out in my first book on this subject, Annette Kolodny, dean of the humanities faculty at the University of Arizona was quoted as saying, "I see my scholarship as an extension of my political activism" (*New York Magazine*, 21 January 1991, p. 36). Since then, I have come across the following "comments."

> We are, ultimately, compelled to choose, to make, express, and act upon our commitments, to denounce the world . . . and above all oppression and whatever arguments have been called upon to validate it. Moreover our speech may well have to be boldly denunciative at times if it is to affect its hearers in the midst of their intellectual and political comfort. (C. H. Knoblauch in "Rhetorical")

> All teaching supposes ideology; there is simply no-value free pedagogy. For these reasons, my paradigm of composition is changing to one of critical literacy, a literacy of political consciousness and social action. (James Laditka in the *Journal of Advanced Composition*)

> We must help our students . . . to engage in a rhetorical process that can collectively generate . . . knowledge and beliefs to displace the repressive

ideologies an unjust social order would prescribe. . . . For instance, [in an experimental composition course he teaches at Purdue] James Berlin might stop trying to be value-neutral and anti-authoritarian in the classroom. Berlin tells his students he is a Marxist but disavows any intention of persuading them to his point of view. Instead, he might openly state that this course aims to promote values of sexual equality and left-oriented labor relations and that this course will challenge students' values insofar as they conflict with these aims. Berlin and his colleagues might openly exert their authority as teachers to try to persuade students to agree with their values instead of pretending that they are merely investigating the nature of sexism and capitalism and leaving the students to draw their own conclusions. (Patricia Bizzell in *College English*)

Teachers need to recognize that methodology alone will not ensure radical visions of the world. An appropriate course content is necessary as well. . . . Equality and democracy are not transcendent values that inevitably emerge when one learns to seek the truth through critical thinking. Rather, if those are the desired values, the teacher must recognize that he or she must influence (perhaps manipulate is the more accurate word) students' values through charisma or power—he or she must accept the role as manipulator. Therefore, it is of course reasonable to try to inculcate into our students the conviction that the dominant order is repressive. (Charles Paine in *College English*)

These statements are quoted in an article by Maxine Hairston entitled "Diversity, Ideology, and Teaching Writing" which appeared in the scholarly journal *College Composition and Communications* in May of 1992. Professor Hairston insists that

These quotations do not represent just a few instances that [she] ferreted out to suit [her] thesis; you will find similar sentiments if you leaf through only a few of the recent issues of *College English*, *Rhetoric Review*, *College Composition and Communication*, *Journal of Advanced Composition*, *Focuses*, and others.

She goes on to say, "At least forty percent of the essays in *The Right to Literacy*, the proceedings of a 1988 conference sponsored by the Modern Language Association in Columbus, Ohio, echo such sentiments" (*College Composition and Communication* 43, May 1992, pp. 180–181).

It is critical to reiterate, that these are quotations from the advocates of politically correct agendas. In other words, Professor Hairston has gone to great lengths to allow the PC crowd to speak for themselves, as I did in my first book on this subject. These are *their own* descriptions of their philosophies, pedagogies, course content, and agendas. And, as I have already mentioned, these people do not stop at pushing their ideologies from the professorial pulpit. They attack and ridicule all other ideologies.

Professor Maxine Hairston laments, "those who advocate such courses [and approaches] show open contempt for their students' values, preferences, or interests" (*College Composition and Communication* 43, May 1992, pp. 180–181). Philip Rieff, professor of sociology at the University of Pennsylvania, would concur. In an interview with *Insight* magazine, Professor Rieff stated, "Students who arrive at universities rooted in a religious faith embedded by family, or who have a moral code they have adopted at their own choosing, are taught that the aim of education is to undermine these givens and show how inadequate they are" (*Insight*, 23 March 1992, p. 36).

Still, in the face of such unequivocal admissions, Catharine Stimpson, and others of her ilk, continue to insist that the whole PC movement is nothing but "a rhetorical strategy by neo-conservatives who have their own agenda." By referring to "anecdotes" of political correctness on campus as "UFO's," Professor Stimpson maintains that PC is nothing but a figment of the paranoid imaginations of "neo-conservatives" who, in her words, "are trying to preserve the supremacy of white, heterosexual males" (*New York Magazine*, 21 January 1993, p. 35).

It is one thing to have an agenda and to pursue it. It is another thing to have an agenda, to pursue it, and deny that there is an agenda or that it is being pursued. To do the former is to exercise one's constitutional right in a free society and is perfectly acceptable. To do the latter is to be intellectually dishonest and would call into serious question the integrity of both those who are capable of resorting to such tactics and the ideas which must be pursued in such a fashion.

Speaking of dishonesty, I must share (a PC thing) an experience that happened to me just prior to the release of my first book on this subject. Professors are expected to travel around the country and attend conferences where we present our research to each other and subject ourselves to the scrutiny and criticism of our peers. In the spring of 1991, I attended the annual conference of the College English Association in Pittsburgh where I did a presentation on my forthcoming book on political correctness.

During my presentation, I quoted Alan Kors, professor of history at the University of Pennsylvania. In referring to the "sensitivity sessions" that the university was beginning to require for students and some faculty, Professor Kors was quoted as saying, "The University of Pennsylvania has become like the University of Peking."

As soon as I had made this comment, a member of the audience interrupted me by raising his hand and asking if he could question me. He was gruff and confrontational. I and, judging by the expressions on the faces of those present, everyone else in the room were stunned. The normal procedure is to allow all the presenters (usually at least half a dozen per session) to finish their presentations before opening the floor for questions. The chair of the session informed the "gentleman" who had so rudely interrupted me of this tradition, with which every academic is, or should be, familiar.

I was allowed to continue without further interruption, and, as soon as the floor was open, this "gentleman" started in on me. He insisted that I was taking quotations out of context and distorting them. He referred specifically to the one by Professor Kors maintaining that "Alan" had not said that. I informed him that my source was the 21 January issue of *New York Magazine*, page thirty-five. My "opponent" then said, "Alan issued a retraction in the *Chronicle of Higher Education*." I specifically remember his referring to Professor Kors by his first name because it left me with the distinct impression that he knew the man.

"Sir," I replied, "first you said that Professor Kors never made the statement. Now you are saying that he issued a retraction. Why would he issue a retraction if he never made the statement?"

My "opponent" never answered my question. In typical PC style, he simply pressed his attack even more aggressively. Dr. Darrell Bourque, a colleague who had accompanied me to the conference and who was present at the session, said that he had never witnessed such rude behavior before and said that he "felt for me." I will admit that I found the episode unnerving and even embarrassing, but I tried to put it out of my mind.

However, when I returned to work, my department head mentioned casually to me that she had heard that I had been confronted in Pittsburgh and accused of misquoting and presenting distorted information. I went straight home and called Professor Kors at the University of Pennsylvania.

I got him on the phone on the first try, read to him the statement that had been attributed to him in *New York Magazine*, and asked him if he had, indeed, made the statement. He said that he had. I asked him if he had later issued a retraction. He said that he had issued a second statement reaffirming in stronger language his original comment. Perhaps I should point out that Alan Kors is the faculty member who defended Eden Jacobowitz, the student at the University of Pennsylvania who was accused of violating the university's "racial-harassment policy" in the now infamous "water buffalo" incident. When I told Professor Kors why I was asking, he was very angry and demanded to know who the person was who had confronted me at the CEA in Pittsburgh. I informed him that I did not know the man's name. My colleague who had accompanied me did say that my "opponent" was some kind of high-ranking official in the MLA, the group which hosts the conference referred to in *U.S. News & World Report* as the "Gong Show of the academic world," where far too many supposed academic presentations are now little more than political diatribes railing against the evils of Western civilization.

Nevertheless, the point of this "anecdote" is that this "gentleman," who was supposed to be a scholar, a professor, and an official in a national academic organization, lied. If Professor Alan Kors can be taken at his word, and I believe he can, then the "gentleman" who confronted me in Pittsburgh at a national conference in front of my colleagues and peers, lied. He obviously did not like what I was saying, so he attacked me, simply making things up as he went along. The problem is that he rattled me. He made me doubt myself and my work in front of an audience of my peers, and, once I had solid evidence that this is what had happened, it was too late. I made a solemn vow to myself that I would never again allow anyone to do that to me.

I learned of a similar incident when I was invited to be the keynote speaker at an academic conference in Dallas in February of 1992. A group of professors from a university in Texas were attempting to stop a revision of the faculty handbook which would specifically prevent "discrimination based on sexual orientation." At a general faculty meeting on this matter, those who were opposed to this move were told that the language that was being proposed for the revised faculty handbook was mandated by federal law. The professors who were opposing the revised language were nonplused and silenced for the moment. After all, that sounds like something the federal government would do. Later, when the professors checked with then Texas senator Lloyd Bentson's office, they were informed that there was no such federal mandate. The professors opposing the revised language for their handbook were successful in preventing that language from being implemented. Still, this "anecdote" is yet another example of the "Make It Up As You Go Along" strategy, undoubtedly effective, but fundamentally dishonest.

I asserted in my first book on this subject that the seeds of the destruction of the PC movement lie within its own hypocrisy and dishonesty. I also maintained that more and more professors were beginning to speak out and to challenge this movement and its proponents and their ideas and tactics and that because of these dissenting voices there was hope that PC and all its attendant "isms" (like multiculturalism, genderism, Afrocentrism, environmentalism, Marxism, etc.) would be exposed for the intellectual frauds that they truly are.

As if to fulfill my prophecy, in April of 1992, the *Chronicle of Higher Education* ran an op-ed piece by Steven Watts, professor of history at the University of Missouri at Columbia, entitled "Academe's Leftists Are Something of a Fraud." In this article, Professor Watts examines the roots of "the intellectual life of *fin-de-siecle* America," i.e., what has come to be called "political correctness." He sees poststructural linguistic theorists "marching steadily, and often frolicking playfully, under the banner of French intellectuals such as Jacques Derrida and Michel Foucault," as having

> joined forces with exhausted remnants of the New Left who are now holed up in university teaching and administrative posts, people who harbor dreams of social revolution fostered in the 1960s. The resulting alliance has produced a curious hybrid—the linguistic left—that has moved to center stage in contemporary academic life.

Professor Watts goes on to accuse the "linguistic left" of being "something of a fraud" for a variety of reasons, not the least of which is that, while posing as revolutionaries supposedly dedicated to the overthrow of the dominant culture which it accuses of being racist, sexist, homophobic, oppressive, and elitist, they themselves have "built a political agenda that is narrowly elitist and overly intellectual." He maintains that this group, while adopting a revolutionary rhetoric, which can clearly be seen in the quotations I cited earlier, these people are nothing more than

> posturing, prosperous academics who like to pretend they are something else. . . . Such attempts to disguise their own social position—an upper-middle-class intelligentsia masking itself as an oppressed group and posing as indispensable figures in the vanguard of revolution—would be laughable if they weren't so earnest.

These "linguistic leftists," Professor Watts continues, occupy "the privileged position of discourse radicals in the modern university," and "from this location its theoretical and political doctrines have emerged as the latest bankrupt expression of radical chic" (*Chronicle*, 29 April 1992, p. A-40). Professor Philip Rieff would again concur and warns, "'The rot always begins at the top,' . . . meaning that societies fall from the faults of their elites, not from the shortcomings of those at the bottom" (*Insight*, 23 March 1992, p. 36). Professor Rieff's reference to the "fall of societies" is a salient point that broadens the scope of the discussion. If the old adage that those who refuse to learn from history are doomed to repeat it is true, then the revision of history, which is so much a part of the "new, PC scholarship," becomes even more alarming in its implications.

Before I go any further, I should reiterate another position I took in my first book on PC, which is that I am not trying to scare people away from college. On the contrary, a college education is becoming increasingly necessary to be marketable in an increasingly competitive, high-tech, fast-paced world. Universities still offer one not only a good education, but a wealth of intellectual and, yes, cultural experiences that are invaluable and well worth the cost of tuition.

Furthermore, as Dr. Gary Marotta, vice-president of academic affairs at the University of Southwestern Louisiana, maintained in an interview he did with me for my first book on this subject, "the great number of American academics command a certain rational middle ground." In other words, the majority of faculty members in most universities are well-educated, thoughtful people with expertise to share.

However, as Dr. Marotta also points out, "What's distressing is those with power who propound extreme ideological points of view which can only be defended with the most contorted kinds of logic and which are always attached to some social goal" are also here at the university. "And they've created a climate," Dr. Marotta continues,

> that does not allow for rational debate. . . . There are dogmatists who have used tenure and promotion to enforce it. . . . They are dangerous people, very dangerous people. Those people are the same as the McCarthyites of the fifties only they dress up in their liberal humanitarian garb, but there is no difference.

He also was quoted in the school newspaper as saying, "In the 1950s the right-wingers were trying to close the door to liberals. Now the other side is trying to close the door" (*The Vermilion*, 26 July 1990, p. 15).

Dr. Marotta is not alone in his assessment of the present situation. Stephan Thernstrom, professor of history at Harvard, also calls the PC movement "a new McCarthyism." Thernstrom goes on to point out that this "is more frightening than the old McCarthyism, which had no support in the academy. Now the enemy is within" (*New York Magazine*, 21 January 1991, p. 37). Sterling Fishman, professor of history and education at the University of Wisconsin, also insists that "it used to be that academic-freedom threats were from the right. But inside the university, they're now coming from the politically correct left" (*Chronicle*, 12 December 1990, p. A-16). Christopher Lasch, professor of history at the University of Rochester, also speaks of "a climate on campuses that is tense and unforgiving" and maintains that "there is a readiness to exclude other points of view because they don't serve the cause of dispossessed groups" (*Chronicle*, 21 November 1990, p. A-14).

Joseph S. Salemi, an adjunct professor of humanities at New York University, maintains that "the voice of the left-liberal orthodoxy is now the loudest, the most raucous, the best financed, and the most dangerous to academic freedom and humane discourse in the humanities." Professor Salemi then points out that "this orthodoxy carries clout—in curriculum revision, in policy matters, in faculty hiring, in grants and awards, and in a thousand details of college life" (*Measure*, January 1992, No. 102, p. 4).

Still, while these grim views of life on campus are all true, I published what could accurately be called an exposé of these conditions, which makes me something akin to a whistle-blower, and, in the spring of 1993, I was recommended by the personnel committee of my department for promotion to associate professor, a recommendation which was accepted by the administration. In the process, I was supported by many colleagues who would identify themselves as political liberals.

I hasten to reiterate in the strongest possible language the position I took in my first book on this subject. One can be a political liberal without being politically correct. In fact, some bonafide political liberals, like Professor David Barber of Duke University and former chairman of Amnesty International, have expressed serious concerns about the politically correct phenomenon that seems very clearly to have come to dominate American college life. My point is that there is still integrity in the university. In spite of the terrorist tactics of some in the PC crowd intended to stifle discussion, the debate goes on, and it is most important.

As Dr. Gary Marotta said, "This discussion and this debate holds the key to the future of liberal arts education. That's what this debate is about. Which way is it going to go? It's the very heart of the matter." I would take issue only with the statement that this debate "holds the key to the future of liberal arts education." I would expand Dr. Marotta's position and maintain that it holds the key to the future of *public* education at all levels. Indeed, the question is, "Which way is it going to go?"

To arrive at some assessment of "which way it is going," I shall begin by discussing where we have come from, the philosophical and intellectual roots of the politically correct phenomenon. I shall then establish where we are with updates on the major "isms" of the politically correct movement, i.e., multiculturalism, Afrocentrism, and genderism (which includes radical feminism and the gay rights movement). Only after this lengthy, fully documented discussion of what is clearly going on will I offer my predictions as to where all this is leading us. As the old, worn-out saying goes, "The journey of a thousand miles begins with a single step." Let us walk together.

Chapter Two

---◇---

PC Roots:
Beyond Sixties Liberalism

As I pointed out in my first book on this subject, John Silber, president of Boston University and a former candidate for governor of the state of Massachusetts, "suggested that higher education was suffering from . . . a profound relativism" that has taken root in our thinking (*Chronicle of Higher Education*, 30 January 1991, p. A-16). I concur with President Silber except that I would say that *all* of education "suffers" from this malady, not just higher education. As I have said many times, when asked a question involving a moral choice, the vast majority of my students respond with two words, "It depends." In their minds, the whole debate on human morality can be accurately summarized and adequately addressed with these two words. The notion is "Who's to say what's morally right? Everyone has his/her own opinion, and who's to say who's right?" It is my position that this "profound relativism" is at the heart of the politically correct phenomenon, which has its roots deeply embedded in "modern" thinking.

Most scholars who have addressed this issue maintain, as I pointed out in my first book on this subject, that
the politically correct phenomenon can be traced back to
the 1960s. Upon more careful consideration, it is my view
that the 1970s must be considered as well. If you can
remember or imagine the most radical student elements
on college campuses during that time and then realize
that many of those student radicals found a home in
academia and are now the teachers and professors and
administrators of our educational system, you will have
some notion of what political correctness is. This comparison, however, is not sufficient.

There can be no denying that the so-called Free Love
and Turn On; Tune In; Drop Out mentality so prevalent
at the time made the sixties and seventies a period of
lasciviousness and that we, those of us who were the foot
soldiers in the "Sexual Revolution," developed a real flair
for rationalizing our self-indulgence. Having admitted that,
it must also be pointed out that the sixties and seventies
were also a time of consciousness raising and intense
spirituality. Anyone who doubts that should read Martin
Luther King's speeches and pay special attention not only
to all the references to God but also to America as a truly
great land with a moral and spiritual heritage. During the
sixties and seventies, America developed its social and
political conscience and proved that it was strong enough
and great enough not only to survive sharp and pointed
criticism but to use such criticism to rise to even greater
heights.

It seems to me that what has come to be called the
politically correct movement has kept the worst of the
sixties and seventies (i.e., the taste for debauchery and
the ability to rationalize lecherous behavior) and has forgotten about or just plain rejected the best that those
times had to offer. In other words, while the PC phenomenon may have its roots in the sixties and seventies, it has
come to violate the spirit of those times.

For example, multiculturalism (or diversity as it is
sometimes called), which is an integral part of the PC

movement, places enormous emphasis on "difference," difference based on ethnicity, race, gender, and even sexual orientation and/or preference. The spirit of the sixties and seventies was that we should be judged not "by the color of our skin but by the content of our character." In other words, things such as race and ethnicity and gender were merely ectoplasmic accidents of birth and, in the final analysis, of no real consequence. The spirit of the sixties and seventies was a call to transcend such superficial differences that separated and divided us so that we might ascend together to that spiritual plateau where we could celebrate our common humanity. That is also the spirit that moves Christianity, at least as I understand it. Considered in these terms, politically correct multiculturalism, which, again, elevates race and ethnicity and gender to the status of religions, flatly contradicts the spirit that informed and moved the sixties and seventies.

In other words, to grasp fully not only what is going on with the politically correct phenomenon but where it all might lead, it is insufficient to say that it has its roots in sixties radicalism. A much broader analysis is needed. As Dr. Burton Raffel, distinguished professor of literature and humanities at my university, suggested in an interview he graciously did with me for my first book on this subject, one must analyze the origins of "modern" thought.

In my view, modern thinking really has its roots in late nineteenth century naturalism, a body of ideas that was shaped, in this country, by the upheavals caused by the Civil War and was based on the writings and teachings of Charles Darwin. The movie *Inherit The Wind*, based on the true story of the so-called Scopes monkey trial, can give some insight as to the controversy caused by Darwin's theories, a controversy that has yet to be resolved. It should also be noted that this trial, which featured former presidential candidate William Jennings Bryan as the principal prosecutor, involved a school teacher refusing to let the state tell him what he could and could not teach. This story, in other words, may be the first bona fide case involving political correctness, but the sides have changed.

At the time of the Scopes "monkey trial," the Bible, specifically the book of Genesis, was the primary text used to teach the origins of the world and of man, and it was actually illegal even to mention Darwin. Now, evolution is taught as indisputable, scientific fact, and it is essentially forbidden to mention the Bible. In other words, as I pointed out in my introduction, the political power has shifted, and those who were once acting as censors are now being censored, and Darwinism has been elevated to the status of a religion that politically incorrect educators challenge at their peril.

Nevertheless, even though it was forbidden by law to discuss such topics as evolution in public classrooms, naturalistic thinking found its way into American literature in the work of writers such as Stephen Crane, Jack London, Frank Norris, and Theodore Dreiser. Consider the following quotation from *Anthology of American Literature: Volume II*, edited by George McMichael, the primary textbook we use at my university for teaching the survey of American literature.

> America's literary naturalists scorned the idea that literature should present comforting moral truths. Instead, naturalistic writers attempted to achieve extreme objectivity and frankness, presenting characters of low social and economic classes who were dominated by their environment and heredity. In presenting the extremes of life, . . . the naturalists emphasized that the world was amoral, that men and women had no free will, that their lives were controlled by heredity and the environment, that religious "truths" were illusory, that the destiny of humanity was misery in life and oblivion in death. (p. 7)

Echoes of the notion that we are "the products of our environment" can surely be heard in the positions taken by the advocates of politically correct multiculturalism. These people would have us believe, for instance, that much if not all criminal behavior is the result of social and economic conditions rather than the result of a conscious choice (free will). From this kind of thinking we get the verdicts and nonverdicts in the trials of the Menendez brothers, Lorena Bobbitt, and those accused of the beating of Reginald Denny. There are even some who are now suggesting that violent, antisocial behavior might be genetically based. Furthermore, the basis of the argument that homosexual behavior is a result of genetics, which is becoming more popular, can also be traced back to the ideas expressed by nineteenth century naturalists.

As I suggested earlier, although what has come to be called "modern" thinking does not really emerge until after World War I, its roots are deeply embedded in late nineteenth century naturalism. Consider the following definition of the "Modern Period" from the *Handbook to Literature* edited by C. Hugh Holman.

> The period that began when World War I blasted the past and history into apparent oblivion. As Matthew Arnold sensed a half a century earlier ("Dover Beach," 1867), the darkling plain was here, in mud and barbed wire, with no joy, love, light, certitude, peace, nor help for pain, where ignorant armies clashed by night. Only a bleak solipsism survived, each sole self projecting its only reality, unsure of its match with any other. The past was dead. God was dead. People were alienated from all community. One could create one's self only by existing, by moving one's existential reality up from the black wall of terror and nothing. . . . Individual consciousness reigned. . . . Emotion and self-will superseded reason and virtue. (p. 295)

This definition of "modernism" and others like it always refer to "existentialism." Although Kierkegaard, a Danish philosopher, "is considered the founder of existentialism," it is the French writer/philosopher Jean-Paul Sartre who provides the intellectual foundation and content for the modern "atheistic branch" of existentialism according to the *Handbook to Literature*. Definitions of existentialism include references to the ideas of "existence before essence," the "impotence of reason," alienation, anxiety, nihilism (nothingness), and "awful freedom."

If I might attempt to simplify this, all the "isms" discussed above, which are the foundation of "modern" thought, move in one direction—inward. With ideas of the absence of God and the "amorality" of the universe together with the notions that society is hopelessly decadent and government hopelessly corrupt taking hold, old, familiar guideposts one was expected to follow are hewn down. There are no certitudes on which to reflect, no absolutes on which to base judgments, no standards by which to measure action. In other words, if I can't count on God or religion or society or government or even other people, what do I have left? The answer is my self.

In my view, modern thought is, beginning with nineteenth century naturalism, a collapse into the *self*. The self becomes the yardstick by which the universe is measured, but only *my* universe because I can't really know anybody else's. This amounts, of course, to a sort of deification of the self. If my self creates its own universe by existing and choosing, then I am the god of a universe of my own making.

It is a very short step from this deification of the self, the end result of existentialism, and the idea that my self is all that I can know, which is the basis of solipsism, to the notion that I must feel good about my self. Sound familiar? After all, if that's all I have, why shouldn't I feel good about it? And so, in the late twentieth century, we have come up with ever more innovative ways to explore our *selves*, to get to know our *selves*, and to come to like our *selves*. This, of course, begins with Freud and the serious study of psychiatry and psychology, at best inexact and still largely theoretical "sciences," and ends with the dime store, politically correct "psychobabble" so rampant in our culture today.

This modern movement "inward," which involves an intense interest in and even a deification of the self, is also a movement toward relativism. If each self creates its own universe by existing and choosing, virtually every-thing becomes a matter of opinion, and all opinions are equal. No one has a right to tell anyone else what to do, to "impose their morality on anyone else." You hear that a lot today. After all, who's to say what morality is?

Now, this kind of thinking may be interesting to de-bate and does hold some charm, especially for rebellious teenagers. It does, after all, give them "permission" to act in any way they choose, and who's to say it's not right? This thinking offers, in other words, incredible freedom, but, as the definition of existentialism states, the freedom is both "awesome and awful," awful because "humans must move forward from black nothing into the moral void by choosing for themselves . . . , creating for them-selves the essence of their being." This is, finally, a fright-ening place to stand, for, in a world without absolutes, there is, as the definition of the "Modern Period" states, "no joy, love, light, certitude, peace, nor help for pain." In other words, if there is only the self, there is nothing and no one to hold on to. There is the self and only the self, alone and alienated, in the darkness of uncertainty.

Welcome to the "modern" world, compliments of the French, the people who gave us the Statue of Liberty, atheistic existentialism, and several venereal diseases. According to the politically correct multiculturalists, I, being of French extraction (as one can tell from my last name), should take pride in my Franco-American heri-tage. My obvious sarcasm, however, makes me very politi-cally incorrect. Oh well, Uh-oh Spaghetti-Os!

The latest "gift" from the French is something called "deconstruction" or "deconstructionism," which I discussed at length in my first book on this subject. Deconstruction-ism is "modern" thinking (this "profound relativism") applied to linguistics. Deconstruction is also referred to as "post-structuralism" (sometimes spelled without the hyphen) or "postmodernism" or "high theory" or just "theory." While there may be some differences between these terms over which some theorist would argue vociferously, rest assured that the differences are so subtle that only an academic would be able to see them or care about them. Jacques Derrida, who teaches at the École des Hautes Études en Science Sociales in Paris, is the French linguist who has been dubbed "the high priest of high theory" by the *Chronicle of Higher Education* (13 October 1993, p. A-9).

According to the *Chronicle of Higher Education*, "Theory is one of those buzz words. . . . Often it is shorthand for the post-structural proposition about the slipperiness of language and the instability of meaning that began to be imported from France in the 1960s" (13 October 1993, p. A-9). According to that same *Chronicle* article, Sheldon Hackney, former president of the University of Pennsylvania (where the now-infamous "water-buffalo incident" occurred), said in his confirmation hearings as Clinton's chairman of the National Endowment for the Humanities (NEH) "that he thought post-structuralism was a form of 'intellectual political correctness.'"

Reduced to their simplest terms, all these "isms" and/ or theories rest on the notion that words have "no inherent meaning." Because different people interpret different words to mean different things, meaning becomes relative. Just as each self creates its own existential world by existing and choosing, each self also creates its own language by the way in which that individual interprets and uses words.

Taken together and to their logical conclusion, these "theories" are an argument for linguistic and intellectual chaos. It reduces the world to a giant Tower of Babel where meaningful communication and understanding are impossible. If the philosophical premises of these "theories" and "isms" are valid, it also means that teachers, and particularly teachers of language, are frauds. If words can mean anything we want them to mean, then a piece of writing can be interpreted in as many different ways as there are people to read it. So, who are we to presume to "teach" literature or anything else? Perhaps we should give back the Statue of Liberty.

However, the politically correct advocates and apologists for these "theories" were not content that this thinking came to dominate academia. According to Frederick Crews, chairman of the English department at the University of California at Berkeley, "in the 1980s, poststructuralism formed a green card marriage with the American left. It latched onto a political content and lingo" (*Chronicle*, 13 October 1993, p. A-17).

A reasonable, thinking person might ask that if this kind of thinking has its roots in nineteenth century naturalism and begins to flower in post World War I Europe (specifically France), why has it taken so long to manifest itself. The answer is that is hasn't. Actually, the twentieth century march into the existential darkness of solipsistic relativism was interrupted.

In my research, I came across an article that included some very compelling statements which are hauntingly relevant to my present discussion. Before I give the specific bibliographical information about this piece, I would like you to consider some of the comments made in this article. Speaking of "the youngsters still in college and the graduates of the past ten years," the writer maintains that "it would be incorrect to speak of the present generation as disillusioned or demoralized. They seem to have grown up without any allegiances that could be betrayed, without a moral philosophy to renounce" (p. 4). When describing "the characteristics of our college-bred youth," the writer speaks of "the disaffection of youth, its distrust of any cause which spoke the language of principles" (p. 5). The writer maintains that at commencement exercises, "stirring phrases would not stir . . . [and] not even the loftiest visions would inspire" (p. 5). The writer then declares, "The real trouble is that our college students and recent graduates do not take *any* moral issues seriously, whether about their personal affairs or the economic and political problems of the nation. Their only principle is that there are no moral principles at all" (p.

7). The writer goes on to state that "their basic distrust is of all statements of principle and conviction, all declarations of moral purpose" (p. 8).

The writer's position is that this is a most unfortunate development and insists that "the calamity has been caused by our schools and colleges" (p. 8). He also maintains that "for the past forty years there have been forces at work in American education which had to culminate in this result" and that "what has been happening in American education. . . , what has finally achieved its full effect in the present generation, flows with tragic inevitability from the seeds of modern culture" (p. 9). Placing the blame for this "calamity" squarely on the heads of the faculty, the writer makes the following points.

> A bright college student will readily draw certain inferences from [the] few basic notions that get dinned into him from every source of his education. He will see for himself that moral questions, questions of good and bad, right and wrong, cannot be answered. . . . He will conclude that "value judgments" cannot be made except of course as expressions of personal prejudice. He will extend this conclusion to cover not only decisions about his own conduct but also moral judgments about economic systems and political programs. He will accept without question the complete divorce of economics from ethics. . . . If, in addition to being bright, he is proud of his modernity, he will regard anyone who talks about standards of goodness, principles of justice, moral virtues as an unregenerate old fogy; and he will express his aversion for such outmoded opinions by the *ad hominem* use of epithets. (p. 11)

Expanding on that point, the writer insists that even students "who are not bright enough to draw their own [politically correct] conclusions from the main tenets of a college education" need not be concerned. They can rest assured that they will "get them ready-made in certain courses." Those "certain courses" are, as one might expect, in the humanities.

> They [students] are told by the teachers of social science that all "systems of morality" reduce to tribal mores, conventional taboos and prescriptions which govern the culture of a given time and place. They learn, as a result of this complete moral relativism, that they must respect their "ethnocentric predicament," which simply means that they, who belong to a given culture or system, cannot judge the right and wrong of any other without begging the question, without taking their own point of view for granted. (p. 11)

This, of course, is precisely the position articulated by the politically correct advocates of multiculturalism. By articulating such positions, they are revealing the "profound relativism" at the root of their thinking.

> To suppose that all men living at any time or place are subject to the same fundamental canons of right and wrong, however diverse their manners or mores; to suppose that all men, precisely because they are all men, sharing equally the same human nature, should be motivated by the same ideals of truth and goodness—that is the demon of absolutism which every social science course in the curriculum tries to exorcise. When they [teachers of social sciences] succeed, as they usually do by sheer weight of unopposed prestige, the college student who has been thus indoctrinated even dislikes using such words as "truth" and "goodness" because they sound like "absolute values." (p. 11)

The writer goes on to point out that it is not only the social science courses that preach this moral relativism. Faculty members in the "philosophy department [also] support the derogation of 'systems of morality' as so many ways of rationalizing emotional fixations and cultural complexes. (Ethics becomes a sort of psychoanalysis.) It is in the philosophy course that the student really learns how to argue . . . against all 'values' as subjective and relative" (p. 12).

The writer also addresses "those who suppose that American colleges are hotbeds of radicalism." He informs the reader that when he and a colleague attempted to teach Karl Marx's *Das Capital* and "tried to show them [the students] how Marx had proved the injustices inherent in the historic processes of capitalism," the students "resisted." "They resisted . . . because they initially rejected the very notion that a moral judgment about capitalism, or anything else, can be proved" (p. 14). In other words, the generation of students about whom the author is writing could not argue *for* anything but could argue against everything. Such is the nature of the "profound relativism" so characteristic of "modern" thinking.

The writer then insists that "the blame [for this] should not fall entirely on the colleges and universities. The corruption begins at the lower levels, long before the student becomes sophisticated in semantics or learns about the ethnocentric predicament" (p. 16). Pointing to "the public school system of the country, at both elementary and secondary levels," the writer maintains that it has been infected with what he calls "pragmatic liberalism—a liberalism 'so completely deflated and debunked' that it forsakes all the 'essential principles of ideal liberalism: justice, freedom, truth' and hence disavows a rationally articulated moral philosophy" (p. 16). He also insists that the men and women who "run" public education in the United States

> have been inoculated with pragmatic liberalism at the leading schools of education (Columbia, Chicago, Harvard, California) where fundamental policies are formed. . . . The mark of indoctrination . . . the marks of the doctrine they had swallowed were the familiar denials—of objectivity of moral standards.

The writer then asks, "If the teachers of the country, and more than the teachers, their higher-ups, are in this state of mind, can we expect the present generation to be otherwise?" (p. 17). He then concludes by maintaining that "those who teach [the] youth are more, immeasurably more influential" than any other individuals in the country.

I have quoted from this writer at such length without telling you his identity or providing you with the bibliographical information about the article for a reason. The preceding comments could easily be taken as a description of the state of education in the United States today. They are not. The author is Mortimer Adler, and the title of the article is "This Prewar Generation." The article first appeared in *Harper's Magazine* in October of 1940. Adler's fear was that the "profound relativism," which had obviously been contracted by "youngsters still in college and the graduates of the past ten years" from the teachers of the day, had left the young people of America "all but disarmed . . . morally" and left them staring at "crises [they were] unprepared to face," namely fascism and nazism.

Adler even relates conversations with faculty members and students who refused to "pass judgment" on the Nazis. "On one occasion . . . an eminent professor of history at the university took the position in after-dinner conversation that, while he didn't *like* Hitler, no one could *prove* that he was wrong" (p. 15). Shortly after the Nazi invasion of the Low Countries, Adler had occasion to converse with two other colleagues who took basically the same position as the "eminent professor of history." One of those colleagues, a professor of international law, told Adler "that his 'preference' for democracy [as opposed to fascism] was simply a cultural bias, arising from 'postulates' which could not themselves be examined for truth or falsity." The other, a professor of medicine, maintained that "each man systematizes his opinions in a certain conceptual frame of reference, there is the democratic frame of reference, the Nazi frame of reference, and so on." Adler then expressed his concern over asking people, and young people in particular, to sacrifice even unto the point of laying down their lives "for a cultural bias, a set of postulates, or a frame of reference" (p. 16).

Adler also spoke of "the contrasting images of Hitler's youth and ours. Of course, Hitler's youth were regimented and hop-fed, but they had some 'virtues' after all. They were loyal and resolute. If only we could generate over-night a faith in democracy that would equal the faith in fascism" (p. 5). In other words, Adler is saying, at least the German youth believed in *something*, and, if our youth had no ideals and principles in which to believe, which is the end result of modern relativism, they just might be at a disadvantage when they had to face Germany's war machine.

Adler then told of a student at Williams College who wrote an editorial that appeared in the campus paper in June of 1940. In that piece, the student asserted,

> The English government and the French govern-ment offer no twentieth-century set of aims and principles in which the poor soldiers in Flanders can put their faith as the German boys put their faith in Hitler. We of the democracies are fighting for next to nothing. It is we, rather than they, who are nihilists. (p. 19)

And, while academics and "intellectuals" engaged in such discussions, the Nazi war machine rolled on.

The *only* way that the forces of fascism would be stopped was if America, the "arsenal of democracy," found the conviction necessary to make the incredible sacrifice that would be required to end the scourge. Fortunately for the whole world and for posterity, we found that conviction, but one cannot help but wonder if we could do it again today. The teachers of today did not "make the world safe for democracy" in 1914 or in 1940. The teachers of today have the legacy of Vietnam. The impli-cations are sobering.

When I said earlier that the twentieth century's march into the darkness of solipsistic relativism had been inter-rupted, I was, of course, referring to World War II. At some point, Americans were forced to draw from deep within their national character and find the moral cour-age to face and fight a clear and present evil. In the process, something else happened. Italian-Americans and German-Americans and Irish-Americans and Jewish-Americans and Spanish-Americans, etc., dropped their hyphens and became Americans. Even black Americans participated and were proud. Though there can be no denying that discrimination and segregation existed in our armed forces at the time, still, blacks saw themselves as Americans with a stake in the fight. Ending the evil of German nazism and Japanese imperialism was more important than protesting the conditions in the military. One can only wonder if World War II will be remembered in history as the last time Americans were able to come together with a sense of moral purpose in a common cause.

I am a firm believer in the notion that the more things change, the more they stay the same, and Adler's article would certainly seem to validate that position. Even though this thinking is called "modern," any serious student of history cannot help but have the nagging feeling that somehow we've seen it all before, even before the twentieth century and even before the nineteenth century. The ideas are complicated, and to understand them would take some degree of sophistication, and becoming intellectually sophisticated is a noble and desirable goal, indeed, the goal of education, right? The root of the word "sophisticated" is "sophist." Throughout his article, Mortimer Adler refers to academics and to the students of his time as "sophists" and to much of their reasoning as "sophistry." It is important and enlightening to know who the original "Sophists" were.

In the fifth century B.C., a school of wandering Greek philosophers who came to be known as "Sophists" appeared on the scene. They concentrated their activities in the cultural center of Athens. According to *Merit Student's Encyclopedia* published by MacMillan and Collier, "The ideas of the Sophists marked a shift of emphasis in philosophy away from earlier cosmological concerns with the natural world [i.e., God and stuff] and toward concern with man and society [i.e., very politically correct]" (Vol. XVII, p. 159). These "new" concerns would make the Sophists early "humanists."

"The Sophists taught that all man's knowledge is based on sensations" (p. 159). In other words, if I can't see it, hear it, smell it, taste it, or feel it, it doesn't exist. The inevitable conclusion, of course, is that God doesn't exist. The Sophists also "taught" that sensations "vary from one person to another and from one time to another" (p. 160). But, if "knowledge is based on sensations" and "sensations vary from one person to another," then knowledge varies from one person to another. But, that's *relativism*, and that was precisely what the ancient Sophists were preaching, and in the fifth century B.C. As I said, the more things change, the more they stay the same.

In fact, Protagorus, "the leading Sophist, taught that 'man is the measure of all things,' that truth is merely opinion, and that, therefore, even morality is relative" (p. 160). Sound familiar? According to the *Encyclopedia Britannica*, the Sophists became known for "their attacks on the traditional religious beliefs" (Vol. XVII, p. 13). They "attacked the traditionally accepted moral code, and . . . they explored and even commended alternative approaches to morality that would condone or allow behavior of a kind inadmissible under the stricter traditional code" (p. 12). Sounds PC to me. The more things change . . .

The champion of "tradition" who dared to oppose the Sophists and their relativism was, of course, Plato. Plato criticized "the Sophistic attack upon traditional values" as "unjustified and unfair." Plato also accused the Sophists of using "'eristic' (Greek *eristikos*, 'fond of wrangling') and 'antilogic'. . . . [Both] involve arguments aimed at victory rather than truth" (p. 11). The more things change . . .

Webster's New World Dictionary defines *sophist* as "1. any group of teachers of rhetoric, politics, philosophy, etc. some of whom were notorious for their clever, specious arguments; 2. a learned person; 3. any person practicing clever, specious reasoning." *Webster's* also defines "sophism" as "a clever, plausible but fallacious argument or form of reasoning." Ready for a real shocker? Consider these definitions, also from *Webster's*, of the word *sophisticate*: "to make impure by mixture or adulteration; to alter without authority, falsify; to corrupt or mislead; to use sophistical reasoning; a sophisticated person."

Interestingly enough, the Sophists were *teachers*; so are PC professors. The Sophists offered instruction in grammar and rhetoric and charged high fees; so do PC professors. Plato charged that the Sophists taught their students that truth was not important. What was important was winning arguments, and winning by any means. Would it be far-fetched to call PC educators modern-day Sophists?

In a piece I cited in my first book on this subject entitled "Ethics Without Virtue," Christiana Hoff Sommers, associate professor of philosophy at Clark University in Massachusetts, levels the same kind of criticism at modern-day professors that Plato leveled at the Sophists and that Mortimer Adler leveled at academics of his time. Professor Sommers "argued that the current style of teaching ethics which concentrated so much on social policy was giving students the wrong ideas about ethics" (*Imprimis*, November 1991, Vol. 20, No. 11, p. 1). She lamented that over and over again on evaluation forms students would say things like, "I learned there was no such thing as right and wrong, just good or bad arguments;" or, "I learned there is no such thing as morality" (p. 2). The more things change . . .

Professor Sommers came to the conclusion that both course content and approach were contributing to the "moral agnosticism and skepticism" of students. When such issues as "abortion, censorship, capital punishment, world hunger, and affirmative action" were discussed in class, Sommers said that she "naturally felt it [her] job to present careful and well-argued positions on all sides." She decided that "this atmosphere of argument and counterargument [what Plato would call "antilogic"] was reinforcing the idea that all moral questions have at least two sides, i.e., that all of ethics is controversial" and "that ethics itself has no solid foundation" (p. 2).

Echoing Adler's concerns, Professor Sommers insists "that we [the professoriate] could be doing a far better job of moral education," and that we should be concerned about teaching our students that "a moral life [is] grounded in something more than personal disposition or political fashion." She goes on to quote Samuel Blumenfeld, who said, "You have to be dead to be value neutral." Sommers also maintains that her response to the question, "Is there really such a thing as moral knowledge?" is an "emphatic 'Yes.' To pretend that we know nothing about basic decency, about human rights, about vice and virtue, is fatuous or disingenuous" (p. 4). She also denounces the position, taken by some professors and educators, that "directive moral education [is] a form of brainwashing," as a "pernicious confusion" (p. 3).

And so, we return to where we began, the late twentieth century and the "profound relativism" of which John Silber spoke. But, obviously, you don't usually find such things as widespread topics of conversation. Only "sophisticated" intellectuals (or those who fancy themselves as such) discuss such matters while sipping wine and nibbling cheese, and one generally finds "sophisticated" intellectuals (pseudo and otherwise) confined in the asylum of academia.

Indeed, it is one thing for professors and "sophisticated" intellectuals to sit around in faculty lounges sipping coffee from stained mugs while they give forth and wax philosophic on such matters. In fact, it is part of the stereotype of the college professor, disheveled, absentminded, living in an ivory tower with little or no meaningful contact with the "real" world, to do such things. And, so long as this mental masturbation is confined to the hallowed halls of academia, it doesn't really bother anybody or threaten anything. But, what happens if the inmates escape? Lock your doors. The inmates did, and some of them went to Washington.

Now for a quick review. The politically correct phenomenon, the intellectual roots of which can be traced all the way back to fifth century B.C. Greece and the Sophists, has its seeds in late nineteenth century naturalism and the ideas of Charles Darwin. These seeds blossom into full-blown "modern" thought as "atheistic existentialism" in post World War I France in the writings and teachings of Jean-Paul Sartre. The darkness of solipsism, nihilism, relativism, anxiety, and despair is deepened by the Great Depression. This darkness is broken temporarily by World War II, which united Americans and our European allies and gave us a sense of moral purpose. The period of optimism and prosperity which followed can, in my view, truly be called America's "Golden Age."

With the Cold War, the threat of nuclear annihilation, the assassination of several of our young, charismatic leaders, and the quagmire of Vietnam, the darkness returned with a vengeance. The "modern" ideas, the intellectual foundation of the politically correct phenomenon, which had been incubating in our universities during and after World War II, reemerged. The adolescence of the movement was on our college campuses during the 1960s. That mindset became institutionalized in our educational system during the seventies, and "in the 1980s, . . . formed a greencard marriage with the American left" and found its way into the mainstream culture through the dominant media and the entertainment industry. The crowning achievement of the movement was the election of Bill Clinton, the draft-dodging, pot-smoking (though not inhaling), womanizing, antiwar, politically correct, Oxford "scholar."

Again, it is one thing for professors and sophisticated intellectuals to discuss strange albeit interesting notions in the confines of the university. It is quite another matter when such people are taken off campuses and placed in positions of power and authority and begin implementing their strange albeit interesting notions as matters of public policy. That is precisely what has happened with Bill Clinton, the PC president, who took up the gay-rights agenda at the Democratic National Convention and tackled the issue of gays in the military as his very first policy initiative.

Clinton actually showed his PC stripes before he took office. As president-elect, he maintained that he would use "diversity" (Clinton's own word) as a litmus for selecting members of his cabinet. And, he was true to his word, which wouldn't be a problem if words meant anything. To a true scholar/intellectual, "diversity" would mean a variety of ideas based, of course, upon the poet William Blake's notion that without contraries there can be no progress. But, in the wonderful modern world of PC deconstruction, words can mean anything you want them to mean, and, alas, for PC sophisticates, the word "diversity" means simply having a certain number of women and members of ethnic minorities and a homosexual or two, even if they all think exactly the same way. And so, Mr. Clinton went back to school and found Donna Shalala, Robert Reich, Lani Guinier, Sheldon Hackney, and other PC professors and made of them a politically correct, elitist vanguard.

Perhaps I misspoke myself earlier when I said that the inmates had escaped. Perhaps it would be more accurate to say that the inmates have taken over the asylum. Oh well, I can invoke the principles of deconstruction and insist that's what I really *meant* to say and just *believe* that I did. As for where it all will lead, I guess we'll just have to stay tuned. As for whether or not there is any hope that we may yet be washed clean of the politically correct infection, I suppose it's possible. But, I believe we'll have to use Whitewater.

Chapter Three

———————◇———————

Multiculturalism:
Beyond the Melting Pot

Have you ever used the word *welsh* to refer to someone's failure to pay up on a bet? If you have, you were not incorrect, linguistically speaking that is. *Webster's New World Dictionary* defines the verb *welsh* as, "to cheat or swindle by failing to pay a bet or other debt," and "to evade (an obligation)." The *American Heritage Dictionary* also defines the verb *welsh* as meaning, "to swindle a person" or "to fail to fulfill an obligation." So, again, if you ever used the word *welsh* in this manner, you would not have been incorrect, until now.

In high Orwellian style, the PC crowd continues its assault on language and words so that now, while using the verb *welsh* to mean "to swindle" or "to fail to meet an obligation" may be linguistically correct, it is politically incorrect because using the word in that manner is "a slur against the people of Wales, says a group known as the Robin Hood Foundation-Welsh American Twm Sion Cati Red Dragon Legal Defense and Education Fund. (Twm Sion Cati is Wales's Robin Hood)" (*U.S. News & World*

Report, 15 March 1993, p. 16). Before you laugh, consider this. According to *U.S. News & World Report*, in March of 1993, this Robin Hood Foundation-Welsh American Twm Sion Cati Red Dragon Legal Defense and Education Fund filed suit in "a Los Angeles court to bar six news organizations, including the *Wall Street Journal* and NBC, from using the word [*welsh*] to mean 'renege.' " Just when you thought it couldn't possibly get any more weird, huh?

The simple fact is that once you begin recognizing this and that group on the basis of ethnicity and/or race and granting those groups all kinds of special protections (including elevating their right not to be offended to the status of a constitutional amendment), you can't stop without being a hypocrite. Why should Welsh-Americans be any less respected and/or protected than African-Americans or Hispanic-Americans or Gay-Americans. That's right, folks. In the wonderful world of politically correct multiculturalism, gays and lesbians are recognized as a specific "cultural" group.

According to Teresa de Laurentis, a professor of the history of consciousness at the University of California at Santa Cruz and a participant in a 1990 conference at that institution called "Queer Theory," "homosexuality [is] not . . . a perversion or an inversion of normal sexual behavior but . . . [is] a cultural form in its own right" (*Chronicle of Higher Education*, 24 October 1990, p. A-6). Anyone for starting a political action committee for monogynous heterosexuals? It seems we could really use a lobbying group for teenage virgins too, which, if you believe the PC media, should belong on the EPA's endangered species list. That group could maintain that the word "condom" is offensive to them and sue to prohibit its use. That, of course, would mean that all the sex education materials in our schools as well as Jocelyn Elders' condom commercials would have to be banned.

As I maintained in my first book on this subject, multiculturalism has been and remains one of the main manifestations of political correctness on and off our campuses. In fact, most of the other PC "isms" are really offshoots of this one. Professor Everette E. Dennis of Columbia University called multiculturalism and political correctness "conceptual companion[s] in the campus debate." He also points out that "political correctness is sometimes regarded as the enforcement arm of multiculturalism" (*War of Words: Freedom of Expression, the University and the Media*, The Freedom Forum Media Studies Center, Columbia University, Fall 1991, pp. 6–7). In my mind, it should be the other way around (i.e., multiculturalism is the enforcement of political correctness), but I won't bicker over details.

As I suggested in chapter 1 of this book, because the phrase "political correctness" has become laughable, it is my view that the PC crowd now refers to themselves more often than not as "multiculturalists" and that such labels as "cultural diversity" have come to replace the phrases "politically correct" or "political correctness" in the campus debates and in the media. Don't be fooled. Only the names are changing. The ideas and the agendas are the same.

You will recall that in the previous chapter, I mentioned "deconstruction," also called "post-structuralism" or "high theory." This is a linguistic theory imported from France based upon ideas of "the slipperiness of language and the instability of meaning," in other words, modern relativism applied to language. Noted scholar Eli Sagan visited my campus in 1992 and delivered a lecture entitled "Cultural Diversity and Moral Relativism." In his remarks, Mr. Sagan made the definitive link between multiculturalism and the "profound relativism," of which John Silber, president of Boston University, spoke and upon which modern and postmodern linguistic theories and, indeed, all of modern thinking rest. Mr. Sagan said,

> It appears that many, if not the vast majority of advocates who are impelling us in the direction of cultural diversity, when faced with the question of whether human morality is universal to all people or merely relative to the society in which it originates, resoundingly come down on the side of

moral relativism. There are no moral universals,
we are told; all morality originates in a particular,
unique society and is, therefore, relative to that
society. There can be no cross-cultural moral discourse, and, most certainly, no culture has the
right to sit in judgment on another culture, because such judgment is grounded, not in some
universal human condition, but merely in the idio-
syncratic cultural position of the particular society
making the judgment.

As I just mentioned, this "profound relativism" is the
philosophical foundation upon which modern and
postmodern thinking rests, and, as I have already pointed
out, "deconstructionism" and/or "post-structuralism" and/
or "postmodern theory" are all various names for this
kind of thinking applied to linguistics. An article in the 13
October 1993 issue of the *Chronicle of Higher Education*
points out that, "theory sometimes refers not just to post-
structuralism, but to any of the 'isms' and schools of
thought that have shaped literary interpretation in the
last 30 years—Marxism, feminism, psychoanalysis, the critical theory of Germany's Frankfurt school," and that "those
approaches to literary criticism are concerned . . . more
with culture [than with literature as literature]" and that
"literary theory has been caught up in the much-publicized culture wars over the humanities" (p. A-16). Michael
Denning, chairman of American studies at Yale and "a
pioneer of cultural studies," concurs and says, "Literary
studies today are interested in how people define themselves—through categories such as race, class, gender, or
ethnicity" (p. A-9).

It is not, however, only literary studies that have been
"caught up in the much-publicized culture wars." According to W. J. T. Mitchell, professor of English at the University of Chicago and editor of the journal *Critical Inquiry*, "The new faces on the block are the new histori-
cism [revision of history], cultural studies, post-colonial-
ism, and gender studies" (*Chronicle*, 13 October 1993, p.
A-9). In other words, what has come to be known as "high

theory" or "post-structuralism," which even Sheldon Hackney, former president of University of Pennsylvania and Bill Clinton's new director of the National Endowment for the Humanities, called "a form of 'intellectual political correctness,'" has thoroughly saturated the humanities.

I *used* to say that such "intellectual political correctness" was confined to the colleges of education and departments of humanities like English, history, political science, sociology, psychology, etc. I used to say that colleges of business and departments of natural science like math, chemistry, biology, etc., had remained uninfected by the virus. I mean, after all, two plus two is four in *any* culture, right? Not any more. The 10 November 1993 issue of the *Chronicle of Higher Education* included on the front page of section two a feature article entitled "Multicultural Science." And, in February of 1993, I was the keynote speaker in Dallas at an academic conference called "Culture Wars on Campus," and it was attended by professors from Texas, Louisiana, Oklahoma, Arkansas, Mississippi, and a few other states in this region. My colleagues from around my region who participated in the conference were mostly from engineering, chemistry, biology, architecture, etc. In other words, most of the academics in attendance were *not* in the humanities, and they assured me that the "culture wars" have definitely spread into their colleges and departments.

To make matters worse, as I have continued to point out, PC thinking is no longer found just on university campuses. In 1991, the New York State Board of Regents convened a task force on minorities, the purpose of which was "purging the state's curriculum of 'Euro-centrism'" (*Boston Herald,* 19 August 1991, p. 23). The chief consultant to this task force, called "the group's guru" by the Boston Herald, was Leonard Jefferies, chair of the department of black studies at City University of New York. There will be much more on Professor Jefferies in the next chapter. Nevertheless, the New York State Board of Regents' Task Force on Minorities prepared and submitted a report entitled "One Nation, Many Peoples."

The report proclaimed that "intellectual and educational oppression . . . has characterized the culture and institutions of the United States and the European American world for centuries." Among other things, the report suggested that "all curricular materials, including those in math and science, be prepared on the basis of multicultural contributions." The result would be that "children from minority cultures will have higher self-esteem and self-respect, while children from European cultures will have a less arrogant perspective" (*New York Magazine*, 21 January 1991, p. 34). Now, a rational, thinking person might be inclined to ask just how cultural differences affect mathematical, biological, and chemical facts and equations. One might also ask just what effect all this concern with kids' "higher self-esteem and self respect" has had on their ACT and SAT scores. These, however, would be rational, logical questions, and, in PC, antilogic is the rule, and power is the endgame.

For evidence of the power of this movement in academia and the extent to which it has gone, one need only consider the proliferation of "sensitivity sessions," speech codes (about which even the ACLU has expressed concern), and highly specialized courses many of which have already become programs of study and some of which are now becoming departments unto themselves. One can now major in African-American studies, women's studies, or gay and lesbian studies. That's right, folks; you can now get a college degree in gay and lesbian studies. I will address each of these areas further in their respective chapters in this book.

However, the multiculturalists are not satisfied with creating whole new, highly specialized departments that are clearly focused on and organized around politically correct ideas. In addition to these new "areas" of study, there are also ongoing efforts to redefine traditional courses, such as freshman English, so that they, too, are politically correct. As I mentioned in my first book on this subject, at my university, I sat on the committee which selected textbooks for freshman English. As a result, I was constantly being sent complimentary copies of texts to review. Consider the following titles and their publishers: *Visions Across the Americas*, Harcourt, Brace, and Jovanovich; *Our Times, Ourselves Among Others*, and *Rereading America: Cultural Contexts for Critical Thinking and Writing*, St. Martin Press; *Encountering Cultures*, Prentice-Hall; *One World, Many Cultures*, MacMillan; *American Mosaic: Multicultural Readings in Context*, Houghton-Miflin; *Cultural Tapestry: Readings for a Pluralistic Society*, Harper-Collins.

These are all texts intended for use as readers in freshman composition courses, and the publishers are all major houses with international distribution which do not even print texts unless they have marketing analyses that indicate a clear and widespread demand. Two specific stories regarding the freshman English programs at two separate universities are enlightening on this matter. I related these stories at length in my first book on this subject, so I shall only summarize them briefly here.

Two freshman writing courses at the University of Massachusetts at Amherst were "revamped . . . so all the readings raise issues of race and social diversity. Since most freshmen are required to take writing, the faculty reasoned, they [the students] would have to deal with those issues" (*Chronicle of Higher Education*, 19 December 1990, p. A-13). The two courses that were "revamped" were Basic Writing and College Writing. The students enrolled in Basic Writing "are required to read and discuss literature in which characters routinely experience some kind of discrimination," while students "in the more advanced College Writing work with materials from periodical and broadcast media that raise issues of diversity" (p. A-13). Marcia S. Curtis, the assistant director of the writing program at the University of Massachusetts at Amherst and the person in charge of the task of compiling the reading list for the "revamped freshman composition courses," said that she specifically did "not want the old canon that is all white, mostly male, and European centered" (p. A-14). There will be more on the "canon" in a moment.

It seemed that "the writing faculty along with faculties in other disciplines, agreed that something had to be done to educate Amherst's predominantly white students about racism" (p. A-13). Please understand that these faculty members are operating from the premise that most of their students are racists, and this is what so many educators, including me, find so deeply offensive about politically correct, multicultural thinking. According to these politically correct academics, all a kid has to do to be presumed, a priori, a racist and a sexist is to be white. This, to me, is profoundly racist.

Nevertheless, the composition faculty at University of Massachusetts decided "to integrate multicultural awareness into freshman composition . . . to provide 'prompts' that encourage students to reflect on their own experiences and deal with their own prejudices" (A-13). Apparently, it was felt that this was also necessary for the faculty, so "sensitivity workshops" are now part of the writing program at the University of Massachusetts at Amherst and are "required for the forty or so new teaching assistants who join the program each year and for faculty members from the English Department who take turns teaching freshman composition" (p. A-14). Anne J. Herrington, associate professor of English and director of the writing program at Amherst, says, "Keeping the focus of freshman composition on racial and social diversity requires continuous vigilance" (A-14).

A series of articles in the Chronicle told the story of a similar move at the University of Texas at Austin. In May of 1990, "an English Department Committee . . . prepared a revised syllabus for a freshman writing course [English 306] that focused on the theme of 'difference.' " This course, which was officially called "Writing About Difference," had, according to Joseph Horn, a professor of psychology at the University of Texas at Austin, "a strongly political message" (*Chronicle*, 21 November 1990, p. A-15).

In fact, critics of the course began calling it "Oppression English" and "a thinly veiled attempt at political indoctrination. Students, they argued, would feel pressured to conform to 'politically correct' views on such issues as sexual discrimination and affirmative action, and would devote more time to learning about oppression than they would about correct sentence structures." The critics of the course also contended that "the proposed readings were consistently leftist" (p. A-15).

The controversy over English 306 at U. T. at Austin even received national attention, and the fall 1990 newsletter of the National Association of Scholars, based at Princeton University, called the move at U. T. "a not-so-subtle attempt to convert a required course into what could be called a 'mass consciousness raising seminar in racism and sexism'" (*Chronicle*, 20 February 1991, p. A-18). Still, in September of 1991, the English department at U. T. voted forty-six to eleven to approve the course.

It is not, however, only freshman English courses that have been targeted by the politically correct advocates of "diversity" and "multicultural awareness." Another story illustrating this point occurred at Wooster College. Again, I discussed this story in detail in my first book on this subject, so I shall summarize briefly here.

In 1989, black students at Wooster College staged a sit-in, demanding a black studies requirement at that school. The "compromise" that was reached with the students was a three-year commitment to change the focus of the required freshman seminar. As a result, the title of the required freshman seminar at Wooster College became "Difference, Power, Discrimination: Perspectives on Race, Gender, Class, and Culture." According to the *Chronicle of Higher Education*, "the course [was] meant to teach the campus's 480 freshmen to think and write critically and focused on racism and sexism in the American Society" (p. A-33).

However, it was also reported that "some students worr[ied] that the seminar, and a related speaker series, establish[ed] a one-sided conversation about political issues on campus" (p. A-33). Others went further and "call[ed] the seminar a lopsided, left-wing attempt to reduce American culture to victims and victimizers. White men especially [said] they [were] too often made the bad guys" (p. A-35).

Jeremiah Jenne, who covered the seminar for the Wooster Voice, the student newspaper, said "the lecture series [was] heavily weighted with liberal speakers" (p. A-35). The editor of the student paper, Mark Osgoode Smith, said that "students feel more oppressed by the political climate the more time they spend at Wooster" (p. A-35). In December of 1991, Douglas L. Miller, a sophomore at Wooster, "announced in the student newspaper that he was leaving the college because of the political climate on the campus," calling the college "a vast laboratory of brain-washing" (p. A-33).

Yet another manifestation of the politically correct moves to "revamp" and "redefine" traditional courses of study to reflect "cultural diversity" and raise "multicultural awareness" can be found in the consistent attacks on the "canon." The "canon" was a list of great books with which students were expected to be familiar in order to be considered educated. One could expect to find on such a list writers like Homer, Plato, Aristotle, Virgil, Chaucer, Shakespeare, Dante, Milton, Wordsworth, Twain, etc. The politically correct position on the great books of Western civilization was articulated by Stanley Hauerwas, a professor at the Divinity School at Duke, who said, "The canon of great literature was created by high-Anglican a——s to underwrite their social class." In other words, it is very chic and politically correct to attack the canon as too white, too male, racist, and sexist and to refer to it as nothing more than "a propaganda exercise to reinforce the notion of white-male superiority" (*New York Magazine*, 21 January 1991, p. 36). Whether the texts that used to be found in the canon had or have any merit beyond the specific circumstances of their composition, whether they, in fact, transcend space and time and speak to all people in all times about the human condition, no longer seems to matter.

Erica Jong, a writer and lecturer, commented on this aspect of the multicultural agenda in the 20 October 1993 issue of the *Chronicle of Higher Education*. She wrote, "It's deeply ironic that those groups previously excluded from the university (poor people, women, people of color) should now be led (by cynical hipsters) to reject the possibility of reading 'Great Books'—indeed, you are not even allowed to use the term, because it implies that all is not relative." Ms. Jong then asks, "Are African-Americans to be allowed to study only their ancestors' myths and legends? Are women to be denied Homer for a steady diet of Catharine MacKinnon?" After "lecturing and guest-teaching" all across the country, Ms. Jong says,

> My impression . . . is that American universities are filled with sourpuss sectarians who judge all books solely on the race and gender of their authors—while, of course, claiming not to judge at all. . . . There is no stress on what is universal in human nature but only a distressing Balkanizing of "texts."

She concludes by saying, "It's sad to see students racing toward the ethnic cleansing of the curriculum under the guise of fairness and multiculturalism. It's still worse to see feminism made an excuse for know-nothingism" (p. B-2). Well said, madam. Well said, indeed.

Linda Gordon, professor of history at the University of Wisconsin at Madison, maintains that it is only "conservative academics who . . . oppose expanding the traditional canon of literary texts and historical topics to include material on previously excluded groups" (*Chronicle*, 16 January 1991, p. A-6). I reiterate my response to Professor Gordon's comments. Speaking as a "conservative academic," I can assure anyone who is interested in the truth that her statement is simply not so, as Ms. Jong's comments also clearly indicate. I have encountered no opposition whatsoever to "expanding the traditional canon," but there is serious opposition to doing away with it altogether. There is also serious resistance to the idea that those of us who profess to be professors of language and literature cannot even come up with a canon. In my view, such a position is an abdication of our responsibility as scholars.

However, let us, for the sake of argument, accept Professor Gordon's rhetoric and give the PC folks the benefit of the doubt and assume that all they are advocating is "expanding the traditional canon of literary texts." For an idea of just what the politically correct multiculturalists would like to include in the list of "great books," consider Rutgers' graduate school dean Catharine Stimpson's "ideal curriculum." She indicated that one book that she would have in her "canon" would be *Stars in My Pocket Like Grains of Sand.* Of this book, Dean Stimpson wrote, "Like many contemporary speculative fictions, *Stars in My Pocket* finds conventional heterosexuality absurd. The central characters are two men, Rat Korga and Marq Dyeth, who have a complex but ecstatic affair" (*New York Magazine,* 21 January 1991, p. 36).

Another example of the politically correct multicultural moves to replace the canon can be found at the University of Arizona, where a new series of humanities courses entitled "Critical Concepts in Western Culture" is now being offered. In this series of courses, "students are examining ideas associated with Western civilization, but they're looking at them from various cultural perspectives." J. Douglas Canfield, a professor of comparative literature at Arizona and the man who developed the first two courses in the series, says, "We developed the sequence as an alternative to the traditional, canonical 'great books' course. We wanted to better understand and critique Western texts by placing them in juxtaposition to popular and non-western culture" (*Chronicle of Higher Education,* 29 May 1991, p. A-9).

As I pointed out in my first book on this subject, there is a very basic problem with Professor Canfield's position. First of all, before one can "better understand and critique Western texts by placing them in juxtaposition to popular and non-western culture," one must first *know* Western texts and Western culture, and that, of course, is the core of the problem. Many, if not most, of our students today are *not* familiar with Western culture *nor* with the "great books" produced by it. Furthermore, not only are the majority of our students unfamiliar with the literature and history of Western civilization, they are hopelessly uninformed about the history of even their own country.

While discussing a particular story in one of the classes that I am teaching this semester, I mentioned the "American Dream." One student raised her hand and asked what that was. When I posed the question to the class, I got the usual politically correct answers about how everyone's dream is different and that there is no one "American Dream." One student said, "Of course, there is. It's Rags to Riches." He, of course, was right. Ironically, the student was from Australia! And, this is the fundamental problem with most of so-called multicultural thinking.

That problem was articulated eloquently by a high-school social studies teacher in New York when she said, "We're trying to teach global culture to ninth graders who have no idea of their own country. I feel they should be well grounded in American history and then integrate the larger knowledge of the world into that" (*Measure*, Nov. 1991, No. 100, p. 1). Again, ironically, this social studies teacher was an immigrant from India. This Indian social studies teacher's comments not only give valuable insight into a fundamental problem being created by "multicultural" approaches to education, but also, once again, underscore my position that the PC virus is no longer confined to college campuses but has infected *all* levels of education. Her statements also point to another discipline that has become a victim of politically correct multiculturalism, i.e. history.

The position being pushed by the politically correct multiculturalists today is that history is no longer and never was "definitive." The idea that history is "a non-biased and accurate reflection of the past is now being shattered by . . . current theories that knowledge is subjective [and, *ipso facto*, relative]," according to Peter Novick, a professor of history at the University of Chicago who wrote and published in 1988 a book entitled *That Noble Dream: The "Objectivity Question" and the American Historical Profession*. The book challenges "the commitment to objectivity" as "the central norm of the profession [of historians]." Professor Novick proclaims, "We should disregard far-reaching claims to objectivity. We don't have to be definitive. We can just be interesting or suggestive" (*Chronicle of Higher Education*, 16 January 1991, p. A-4).

In that same issue of the *Chronicle*, Linda Gordon, professor of history at the University of Wisconsin at Madison (whom I mentioned earlier), echoes Mr. Novick's position and maintains that "the most interesting debates in scholarship today are not at heart about objectivity and the nature of historical knowledge, but about politics. Political agendas," she continues, "are the real determinants of different approaches to writing history today" (p. A-5).

Again, unfortunately, what began in our colleges and universities has percolated down so that it now is found throughout the entire educational system. Lawrence Auster, a free-lance writer, was on hand at the New York State Board of Regents meeting when the Regents' task force on minorities submitted its report entitled "One Nation, Many Peoples." His observations are illustrative of what is going on and has been going on for some time. Again, I spoke in detail on this in my first book on this subject, so I shall briefly summarize here.

After sitting through the entire meeting of the Regents, Mr. Auster was left with the impression that the new curriculum "has nothing to do with knowledge as it is normally understood, but with the contemporary version of 'morality,' . . . [and that] the emphasis on 'moral perspectives' also places in an even-more alarming light the proposal to downplay historical information." Auster concluded that, "multiculturalism is not about 'understanding different cultures,' as it claims, but about pushing an alienated view of American culture and history" and that "an 'adequate' curriculum was defined by the [New York] Regents as one which showed 'enough' shameful things about our past." Auster then quoted one commissioner who said, "We don't need textbooks on World War II. We only need to ask one question: Why was the bomb dropped?" (*Measure*, Nov. 1991, No. 100, pp. 3-4).

ABC's "Nightline" dedicated an entire program to the effects of politically correct multiculturalism on the instruction of history. Patricia Geyer appeared on the program. A school teacher for twenty-five years, Ms. Geyer is presently teaching world history and economics at the West Campus of Johnson High School in Sacramento, California. She admitted on that show that she "teaches history differently now than [she] used to ten years ago." Ms. Geyer said that she has changed the way she teaches World War II, for instance because her "clientele has changed." Her "clientele" are her students. Ms. Geyer said that, "When we talked about World War II, we gave the official story. . . . Now I have to say: 'How did the Japanese feel about this? Why did they do these things? What were their reasons?' " Ms. Geyer also said on that program that, "History is what is important to you."

Two questions might pop into the mind of a rational, analytical person in response to Ms. Geyer's comments. First, isn't she being a bit presumptuous in pretending that she could ever know the answers to any of the questions she posed? After all, the multicultural apologists are very fond of saying things like: "Men just don't get it" or "White people just don't get it." Ms. Geyer is white, so how could she ever "get" the Japanese perspective. Secondly, is there any truth to the scriptural passage, "The tree shall be known by its fruit"? Why is it not enough to study what the Japanese *did* during World War II rather than trying to determine how they *felt*?

But, alas, even the story of World War II, that Herculean struggle that interrupted the twentieth century's march toward relativistic darkness and united us (possibly for the last time) in a common cause to defeat something that was widely perceived to be evil, is now being revised by the politically correct multiculturalists to reflect the "perspectives" of the aggressors. How interesting, and how far are we to go with this new notion of history?

Former secretary of education William Bennett also appeared on the "Nightline" program and gave an indication of just how far all this has already gone. Mr. Bennett said, "I saw in the context of the Pearl Harbor discussion [during the 50th anniversary of the bombing] a group of students who were talking about Pearl Harbor and World War II, and one of them said, 'Well, I understand our conduct during that war was racist, but at least it wasn't sexist.' " How interesting.

Fortunately, these politically correct notions have not gone unchallenged in academia. For instance, the New York Board of Regents' report led

> a group of prominent historians—including several past presidents of prestigious scholarly associations—[to] issue a widely publicized statement that attacked [the] New York State curriculum report ["One Nation, Many Peoples"] for "ethnic cheerleading" and for violating "commonly accepted standards of evidence" in the study of history. (*Chronicle of Higher Education*, 6 February 1991, p. A-6)

Dr. Gary Marotta, professor of history and academic vice-president of my university, also addressed this whole issue of revising history to suit cultural perspectives and "political agendas" in an interview he did with me for my first book on this subject. He said, "Those who advocate such positions [as Ms. Geyer and Professors Novick and Gordon] are the historical equivalents of literary critics who subscribe to deconstructionism. They say: 'There is no truth,' and, 'We can never know truth wholly.' " Dr. Marotta rejects this kind of thinking and maintains, "We must believe in truth, and we must believe in objectivity even though we know we cannot fully describe it or fully achieve it. To say there is none, then that gives merit to the notion that everything can be manipulated."

Joan Hoff, professor of history at Indiana, concurs with Dr. Marotta and also suggests that the marriage of "poststructural" linguistic theories and history is, at best, an uneasy one. She maintains that, "post-structural theory is hostile to the basic concept of linear time and of cause and effect, which are so characteristic of history as a discipline." Professor Hoff asserts that, "Like all postmodern theories, poststructuralism casts stable meanings into doubt. It sees language as so slippery that it compromises historians' ability to identify facts and chronological narratives" (*Chronicle of Higher Education*, 20 October 1993, p. B-1). Because of this, she concludes that, "Poststructuralism [or 'postmodern theories' or 'deconstructionism' or whatever we choose to call it] cannot under any circumstances be considered 'history friendly.' " (p. B-2).

Professor Hoff is also coeditor of the *Journal of Women's History* and also expresses concerns over problems "poststructuralism" poses for "women's history" specifically. She taught at the University of Warsaw and at University College Dublin, and it was when she spent two years teaching and studying outside of this country that she became "alerted" to what she calls this "serious threat facing women's history in the United States: the overreliance on an American brand of postmodern theory originally derived from France." She criticizes "women's historians in the United States [who] have come to rely heavily on a range of linguistic theories often known collectively as post-structuralism." Professor Hoff also sees

> the trendy theory as irrelevant or even counterproductive . . . [in that] this kind of post-structuralism is already beginning to isolate women's history . . . from the women's movement, . . . from history teachers trying to integrate material on women into their classes, . . . [and] U. S. scholars in women's history from their counterparts abroad.

Furthermore, and this is the main problem, "it [poststructural theory] reduces to mere subjective stories the experiences of women struggling to define themselves in particular historical contexts" (p. B–2).

Professor Hoff's point, however, applies not just to "women's history," but to *all* of history because, given the "poststructural" philosophical positions, the "experiences" of *all* people "struggling to define themselves in particular historical contexts" are "reduced to mere subjective stories," colored by the peculiar and specific "cultural perspective." In other words, do we teach the Holocaust from the Nazi perspective? Ms. Geyer would have to if she is to be consistent. And, what about Professors Novick and Gordon who inform us that history can be "suggestive and interesting" rather than "definitive and objective" and that "political agendas are the real determinants of writing history." Would they be willing to recognize the legitimacy of the "perspective" that the Holocaust was either greatly exaggerated or that it never happened at all? If they are not willing to do so, then they will, in effect, have admitted that their premise is false.

Deborah Lipstadt addresses these very issues in her recent book, *Denying the Holocaust.* Ms. Lipstadt is "appalled by the willingness of some students [and faculty] and the media to see Holocaust denial as simply 'the other side.' . . . In this relativistic time we live in, Holocaust denial is turned into an opinion, and everyone's opinion is of equal validity. That's like asking whether slavery happened" (*Newsweek*, 20 December 1993, p. 120). Considered in this context, the positions of people like Peter Novick, Linda Gordon, and Patricia Geyer are not only a violation "of commonly accepted standards of evidence in the study of history" and an intellectual "fraud" (as Steven Watts, professor of history at the University of Missouri at Columbia refers to "the linguistic left" and their disciples in other disciplines), they are dangerous, very dangerous, indeed. As Professor Diane Ravitch of Columbia points out, "By promoting a brand of history in which everyone is either a descendant of victims or oppressors [which is exactly what poststructural, new-historicist approaches do], ancient hatreds are fanned and re-created in each new generation" (*New York Magazine*, 21 January 1991, p. 40). Still, this politically correct multiculturalism, with all its inherent problems, is still all the rage on campus. Consider the following examples.

In September of 1992, the *Wall Street Journal* featured what could be called a "back-to-school" piece entitled "Welcome, Freshman! Oppressor or Oppressed?" According to Heather MacDonald, the author of this article and a lawyer living in New York, "Within days of arrival on campus, 'new students' (the euphemism of choice for 'freshmen' [That gets the 'men' out of 'freshmen'; get it?]) learn the paramount role of gender, race, ethnicity, class and sexual orientation in determining their own and others' identity." Ms. MacDonald points out that, "An informal survey shows that two themes predominate at freshmen orientation programs—oppression and difference—foreshadowing leitmotifs of the coming four years."

As an example, she points to the University of California at Berkeley which, for the 1992 fall semester, "changed the focus of its freshman orientation from 'stereotyping' to 'racism, homophobia, status-ism, sexism, and age-ism.'" The reason for the change, according to Michele Frasier, assistant director of the new student program at Berkeley, was that "the program organizers 'wanted to talk more specifically about specific issues the students will face . . . [and] to make students aware of the issues they need to think about, so they're not surprised when they face them.'"

Dartmouth featured a "mandatory program for freshmen" (or "new students" if you prefer the politically correct euphemism) called "Social Issues." According to Tony Tillman, assistant dean of freshmen, as part of the program, skits were presented on "'the issues first year students face,' which he defined as 'the various forms of isms': sexism, racism, classism, etc.'" Apparently, the content of some of the skits "overlapped" because, according to Tillman, "discrimination cannot be compartmentalized: 'It's not as if today, I have a racist experience, tomorrow, a sexist [one]. In any one day, one may be up against several issues. Some issues of sexism have a racist foundation, and vice versa."

Oberlin College also "shows its new students a performance piece on 'differences in race, ethnicity, sexuality, gender, and culture.'" This "performance piece" is "follow[ed] up with separate orientation programs for Asian-Americans, blacks, Latinos, and gay, lesbian and bisexual students." At Stanford, freshmen observed a program entitled "Faces of Community," which was "a panel of students and staff who each embodied some officially recognized difference." The assistant to the president for multicultural programs at Bowdin "hosted a brown-bag lunch for freshmen entitled 'Defining Diversity: Your Role in Racial-Consciousness Raising, Cultural Differences, and Cross-Cultural Social Enhancers.'"

Duke University, which has been a hotbed of political correctness for some time, "got a head start on its mission. Over the summer, it sent each freshman a glossy booklet entitled, 'A Vision for Duke,' which included full-page photos of scrupulously diverse groups of students." The package also reportedly included a letter from H. Keith H. Brodie, the president of Duke. According to the *Wall Street Journal* article, this

> letter leaves no doubt that multiculturalism is not
> an optional occupation at Duke. It crisply informs
> each student that, after listening to a speech by
> Maya Angelou, you and your classmates will en-
> gage in a discussion of questions raised by Ms.
> Angelou and by the enclosed booklet.

At Columbia University, "freshmen heard three of their classmates read essays on what being different—gay, black and Asian-American—had meant in their lives." Assistant Dean Michael Fenlon was quoted as saying, "the goal is to initiate an awareness of difference and the implications of difference for the Columbia community." Dean Fenlon also emphasized that, "this is not a one-shot program. We expect it will continue through their four years here, not just in the classrooms, but in the residence halls, on the playing fields, and in every aspect of student life." Kathryn Balmer, assistant dean of freshmen at Columbia, said, "you can't bring all these people together and say, 'Now be one big happy community,' without some sort of training. . . . It isn't an ideal world, so we need to do some education." Ms. MacDonald, the author of the piece, points out that "students have somehow managed for years to form a college community in the absence of such 'education' [and training] has apparently escaped administrative attention." One might also ask whether or not it would have been more appropriate for Dean Balmer to use the word "re-education," i.e., indoctrination. This leads to one of Ms. MacDonald's salient closing points: "Today's freshman orientations, prelude to the education to come, raise one of the great unexplained mysteries of our time: how the obsessive emphasis on 'difference' and victimization will lead to a more unified, harmonious culture." The obvious, logical response to Ms. MacDonald's very legitimate question is, "It won't!" Still, the politically correct multicultural beat goes on.

According to the spring 1992 issue of *Campus* magazine, 72 percent of four-year, public universities have introduced "multicultural changes" into their curriculum, and 54 percent now have a multicultural requirement. In the fall of 1993, the American Council on Education issued a four hundred-page directory entitled *Sources: Diversity Initiatives in Higher Education* which "provides a state-by-state, campus-by-campus listing of more than 2,000 curriculum projects, faculty-development programs, and student-requirement efforts. It lists more than 225 books, reports, and other publications on multicultural education and related issues" (*Chronicle of Higher Education*, 11 November 1993, p. A-17). Perhaps it is clear why Jerry G. Gaff, a senior staff member of the Association of American Colleges and a senior fellow at the University of Minnesota's School of Education, recently lamented in an article that appeared in *Change*, which is published by the American Association of Higher Education, "The multicultural wars remain a hot topic in the press, but on campus, the war is over: Multiculturalism won" (*Campus*, Spring 1992, p. 9). As proof of Mr. Gaff's position, consider the following "anecdotes."

York College, part of the City University of New York system, adopted a "multicultural requirement. . . . Students must take a course on multiculturalism in the United States, one on a particular region of the world, and one on Western civilization" (*Chronicle*, 21 April 1993, p. A-15). Some herald such requirements as "giv[ing] Western culture an unexpected boost" because York had no Western-culture requirement before. Perhaps, but what if the Western-culture course is taught by a PC prof? As Ronald Darby, a professor of chemical engineering at Texas A & M pointed out, "A lot of these people who teach these courses have a bone to pick or an agenda to advance" (*Chronicle*, 17 November 1993, p. A-23).

Hunter College, also part of the City University of New York system, also recently adopted a "pluralism" requirement. To fulfill the requirement, a student will be required to take four courses. "Along with courses that examine non-European cultures, American minority groups, and gender or sexual orientation, students will be required to take a course on intellectual traditions derived from Europe" (*Chronicle*, 21 April 1993, p. A-13). Did you catch that? That's *one* course on "intellectual traditions derived from Europe," one out of four. Considering Europe's dominance, that seems fair, doesn't it? And, again, what if the one course a student takes on the "intellectual traditions derived from Europe" is taught by a PC prof with "a bone to pick or an agenda to advance"? But, hold on, folks. That wasn't the problem that arose at Hunter College.

It seems that during the debate over the "pluralism" requirement at Hunter, "a heated discussion ensued over whether perspectives on disabled people should be included" (*Chronicle*, p. A-15). That's right, folks; we now have advocates for "disability studies." Simi Linton, an educational psychologist at Hunter, "defines disability studies as an emerging academic subfield that attempts to examine the social construction of the disabled in the same way that women's studies looks at gender" (p. A-15). This proposal reportedly prompted "some of the strongest advocates of the pluralism plan" to take the position that "requiring 'disability studies' would have meant caving in to exactly the kind of political pressure that the right has argued is so widespread." Ms. Linton responded, "My question was . . . by what criteria were some areas of scholarship excluded? I'm not sure I got a good answer" (p. A-15).

That's because there *is* no "good answer" to Ms. Linton's question. The simple fact is that once you start skipping down the politically correct road, there is no turning back or stopping, and excluding "disability studies" while allowing gay studies is inconsistent and hypocritical. The solution is not to "cave in" to *any* of the political pressure of any of these special interest groups that are Balkanizing our system of education. That, of course, is now out of the question because the "caving in" to all the special interest groups has already done serious damage to the educational system in this country. One can only hope that the damage is not irreparable.

One of the positive things multiculturalism does, however, is open up whole new worlds for research in virtually every discipline, and in the university, where "publish or perish" is still the rule, that attracts professors like honey attracts flies. The latest victim in the expanding field of "multicultural" research is, believe it or not, *National Geographic*.

Two cultural anthropologists have written a book entitled *Reading National Geographic* in which the claim is made that, "Taken as a whole, the images in the magazine tend to idealize and portray third-world peoples as exotic while playing down evidence of poverty and violence" (*Chronicle of Higher Education*, 6 October 1993, p. A-10). Catherine A. Lutz, an associate professor of anthropology at the University of North Carolina at Chapel Hill, and Jane L. Collins, an associate professor of sociology at the University of Wisconsin, randomly selected six hundred pictures from *National Geographic* issues dating from 1950 to 1986, "analyzing them for what the photographs said about race, gender and modernity" (p. A-10). Professors Lutz and Collins concluded that the images tell us "that the third world is a safe place [and] that it is made up of people basically like us." They also "argue that the photographs of naked black women . . . conform to Western myths about black women's sexuality, namely that a lack of modesty places black women closer to nature" (p. A-13). It sounds like *National Geographic* is being accused of racism, sexism, and cultural bias.

One might ask just what Professors Lutz and Collins would have *National Geographic* do? Is the magazine not showing "indigenous peoples" in their natural settings? One might ask how that is making photographs "conform to Western myths." Should the *National Geographic* photographers have these women dress up in costumes? But, wouldn't that be making the photographs "conform to Western myths" of decorum and modesty, not to mention lying? The point is that no matter what *National Geographic* chose to do, Professors Lutz and Collins could have written a book criticizing them, and that is typical of political correctness. The obvious solution is to ban the publication of *National Geographic*.

As if it were not bad enough that a publication as distinguished as *National Geographic* is now being attacked, these kinds of sensitivities have even reached the hallowed halls of the Smithsonian Institute. According to the *Wall Street Journal*, Robert Sullivan, one of the Smithsonian's associate directors, maintains that the museum's "permanent exhibits are in a 'crisis' and woefully out of date." He criticizes many of the exhibits for "exoticizing cultures" and maintains that "reforms are long overdue." Mr. Sullivan said to the *Journal*, "The folks who were brought up with [ideas of] fairness in the '60s [the PC crowd] have a sense of civil rights and gender rights. . . . We've got a mandate. Museums are being redefined by principles of pluralism, cultural equity and ecology." In order to achieve these goals, Mr. Sullivan has "targeted" exhibits that display "sexual and cultural inequity."

In order to facilitate "targeting sexual and cultural inequity in the museum," Associate Director Sullivan "has created a secret group of museum employees called 'the dirty dozen,' modeled after a 1967 macho movie in which actor Lee Marvin leads a band of convicts behind enemy lines during World War II." One of the exhibits that has already fallen victim to Sullivan's "dirty dozen" mentality was "an exhibit of Capt. John Smith trading with Powhatan Indians on the James River in 1607." In that exhibit, "Capt. Smith stands in a commanding pose on his boat as a bare-breasted Powhatan woman gazes adoringly up at him from a canoe." What's wrong with that, you might ask? Isn't that an accurate depiction of what happened? "Probably not!" Sullivan's "dirty dozen" would surely shout. And, even if it is accurate, it doesn't matter because, according to Sullivan, "It's sexist."

Another exhibit targeted "is one of the museum's most popular exhibits: a leaping Indian tiger in the mammal hall." Sullivan told the *Journal* that he does not approve of some of the pictures taken near the exhibit.

> Mr. Sullivan, 43, mockingly grits his teeth and flexes his muscles, showing how many men pose for snapshots by the tiger. It irks him. "There's a longstanding human tradition to create a myth around animals as a justification for wiping them out," he says. (*Wall Street Journal*, 29 September 1992, p. 1)

What next? Just what, you might ask, are the limits of politically correct "sensitivity"?

Perhaps the silliest and most publicized manifestation of the politically correct child of multiculturalism, the "constitutional right not to be offended" syndrome, is in the continuing assault on sports mascots. For instance, the song "Dixie" is under attack as a racist leftover of slavery. The Confederate flag has also come under assault at virtually every institution where it is flown, including Utah's Dixie College, even though Utah was never a slave-owning territory. According to the *Chronicle of Higher Education*,

> Dixie College, in Utah, ... got its name because it is situated in the southwest corner of the state, in a temperate region once known for producing cotton. ... For decades Dixie College has flown the Confederate battle flag during football games.

In the fall of 1993, "Student representatives . . . voted ... to abandon it ... [although] the football team will remain 'the Rebels,' and their mascot will still be 'Rodney Rebel'—for now, anyway" (10 November 1993, p. A-33).

That same article in the *Chronicle* also reported of a similar situation at Auburn. "Sports teams at Auburn University at Montgomery . . . have been known as the 'Senators' since the founding of the institution in 1967. Logos depicting the Senator since then . . . all showed Caucasian, gentlemanly, Robert-E.-Lee-esque figures." Last spring, the University unveiled a new Senator character, and " 'some people said he looked like Colonel Sanders, or some plantation owner,' says Terrence A. Adams, a senior who is the student-government president." When a referendum, organized by "student leaders," was held, "a majority of students voted against the existing mascot. . . . Mr. Adams says his goal is to find a new name and mascot that 'won't be sexist or racist, and that won't offend any group of people' " (p. A-33). Good luck, Mr. Adams.

According to the same *Chronicle of Higher Education* article, the University of Alabama invested "over a year of study and $18,000" to come up with " 'Blaze,' a cartoonish Nordic warrior with a big dimple in his chin and a mouth open in a war cry." As you might expect, complaints started coming in, "first . . . from some women on campus, then from a few minority students." Mike Ellis, a university spokesman described the objections to Blaze as "sort of a general grumbling." Blaze is no longer the University of Alabama's mascot, and "the main reason he's gone is that students at the . . . Birmingham campus thought he was too Teutonic—and too aggressively masculine—to represent them" (p. A-33).

Perhaps the single most well-publicized incident involving mascots was at the University of Massachusetts. Objections were raised to that university's mascot, the Minuteman. The objections were that the Minuteman "is a white, male symbol of violence that should be abolished" (*Chronicle of Higher Education*, 27 October 1993, p. A-4). Martin Jones, a junior at the University of Massachusetts who brought the petition against the Minuteman, said,

> "It is the image itself . . . that is the problem. To have a white male represent a student body that is

not exclusively white or male is culturally biased, and promotes racism." He also question[ed] the appropriateness of having a "military figure" representing a campus devoted to intellectual inquiry. (*Chronicle*, 10 November 1993, p. A-33)

According to that *Chronicle* story, when the chancellor of the University of Massachusetts, David K. Scott, "pulled the plug on the Minuteman debate," Mr. Jones went on a hunger strike. "It lasted four days, ending when the chancellor, Mr. Jones, and Mr. Jones's mother went out for Italian food." I wonder who picked up the tab.

Images of and nicknames for Native Americans have also drawn much fire. The *Chronicle* reported in its 27 October 1993 issue that when the University of Iowa played the University of Illinois in football last year, the student-run homecoming council at the University of Iowa banned "images of Indians" from the University of Iowa campus. It was reported that "images of American Indians" were prohibited in all homecoming displays because "American Indians were offended." In the 10 November 1993 issue of the *Chronicle*, it was reported that the homecoming committee at the University of Illinois issued a similar ban on all homecoming floats. Now, the University of Illinois football team is called the "Fighting Illini" and the mascot is "Chief Illiniwek." Coming up with homecoming displays and floats *without* "images of American Indians" would, therefore, pose an interesting problem for students at *both* campuses. But, this is college, so I guess it became an exercise in creativity.

It was also reported in the *Chronicle* that

Marquette University announced last month [October 1993] that it was dropping its team name, "the Warriors," as well as the Indian logo that went with it. "The University has a very strong mission," says Bill Cords, Marquette's director of athletics. "Part of that mission is to show respect for others, and not to create differences among people." (10 November 1993, p. A-35)

But, wait a minute! All politically correct multiculturalism does is talk about "differences." Nevertheless, the *Chronicle* also reported on 20 October 1993 that "Marquette's teams will no longer be known as the Warriors . . . because of concerns that the use of American Indian names, symbols, and images trivializes American Indian culture."

Professional sports franchises have also come under attack for the names of their teams, like the Washington Redskins, the Kansas City Chiefs, and the Atlanta Braves. The now-infamous "Tomahawk Chop" cheer, used by fans of the Kansas City Chiefs, the Atlanta Braves, and the Florida State Seminoles, has also been criticized. According to the *Chronicle*, other schools that have succumbed to politically correct pressure regarding the names and/or mascots of their sports teams include the Arkansas State University Indians who "put [their] mascot, 'Runnin' Joe,' to rest" and the Bradley University Braves who "replaced [their] tomahawk-wielding Indian mascot with a bobcat" (10 November 1993, p. A-35). Unfortunately, that, too, has its risks. As pointed out in the *Chronicle*, "Adopting an animal as a mascot, however, hardly means the end of public-relations nightmares" (10 November 1993, p. A-35).

As Roderick Nash, a professor at the University of California at Santa Barbara, pointed out "during a lecture on environmental ethics, there is a movement to start referring to pets as animal companions. (Apparently, domesticated animals are offended by the word *pet*.) Nash then made some sort of off-the-cuff observation about how women who pose for *Penthouse* are still called Pets (and not *Penthouse* Animal Companions)" (*New York Magazine*, 21 January 1991, p. 37). Of course, "several female students filed a formal sexual-harassment complaint against him [Professor Nash]" for his "off-the-cuff observation."

With these kinds of "sensitivities" rampant in our society today, how far are we from adding "specieism," oppression of animals by people, to the list of officially recognized categories of oppression? Hasn't the animal rights movement already come close to doing this? Would it surprise anyone that People for the Ethical Treatment of Animals has criticized schools that use animals as mascots and have a real animal that is kept at the university and brought out during sporting events? Kim Roberts, an animal-cruelty caseworker with PETA, says, "If someone wants to dress up as a bird, that's fine. But I don't see any justifiable reason to keep a real animal" (*Chronicle*, 10 November 1993, p. A-35). Notice that Roberts does not qualify the position at all. That means that even if the animal is well cared for, it's still unacceptable to keep it. So much for pets.

Even if one were inclined to concede Roberts' point, consider the story about the Kennesaw State College "Fighting Owls," who according to the *Chronicle*, "for years had the informal nickname 'the Hooters.' In the late 1980s, the college named its basketball arena the 'Hooterdome' and its baseball stadium 'Hooter Field,' " (10 November 1993, p. A-35). Wanna guess where this is going to go? As you might expect, "the college decided to drop the nickname" because, according to a spokeswoman, "The term had come to mean something besides owls."

Even parking at sporting events must be careful to not to offend politically correct multicultural sensitivities. According to *Newsweek*, the Texas Rangers baseball club, in an effort to "jazz up the parking areas at its new stadium in Arlington," decided to "name parking areas after Texas heroes, complete with portrait signs and biographies." Sounds like a good marketing idea, but, alas, all the "Texas heroes" featured in the parking lot except one are, you guessed it, white men, like Sam Houston and Davy Crockett. A formal complaint was apparently filed by the Texas African-American Organization. David Williams, a representative of that group, reportedly said, "It's time to be inclusive when it comes to the history of Texas." Even the *Chronicle of Higher Education* admits that in "the push for greater inclusiveness . . . many are having a tough time keeping up with changing mores as [we] evaluate" all these things that seem, at worst, "often inane" (10 November 1993, p. A-33).

We also had problems with the mascot at my university, the University of Southwestern Louisiana. The school is located in Lafayette, the heart of Acadiana, "Cajun" country. And so, our sports teams came to be called the "Ragin' Cajuns." Why not? It has a nice ring to it, and it would appear, at first glance, to be politically correct. I mean, if one is a disciple of "multiculturalism," why shouldn't Cajuns be allowed to celebrate their culture like all the other ethnic minorities which are demanding special political consideration these days? Our people were cast out of their native land, and our parents and grandparents were looked down upon and called by racial epithets like "coonass." The oppression of Cajuns even went to the extreme of prohibiting kids from speaking French at school. If the kids forgot and did speak French, they were disciplined, often physically. Wouldn't that qualify my people, the Cajuns, as an "oppressed minority" and make them deserving of politically correct sympathy. That, of course, is logically consistent with the positions taken by the PC crowd *themselves*. But, as I have pointed out, in the wonderful world of PC, *anti*logic prevails. To identify yourself as an ethnic minority these days means you actually have to enter a competition for "Most Favored Victim Status."

Black students at USL objected to the designation "Ragin' Cajuns" for our sports teams. Among the objections that were published in the *Vermilion*, our campus newspaper, was this: the word *Ragin* spelled backward *is a racial slur*! No kidding. Somebody actually said that. It doesn't matter at all that the word "Ragin" spelled backward is *not even a word*, racial or otherwise.

As I said in my introductory chapter, one of the positive effects of the whole politically correct movement has been to remind us of the power of words to hurt. No decent, thinking human being desires to inflict pain on others, not even inadvertently. But, when people start spelling words backward to "unveil hidden racist agendas," even the most "sensitive" of individuals just might be tempted to roll his/her eyes and sigh, "Oh please." But, believe it or not, it gets worse. The *Chronicle of Higher Education*'s 21 April 1993 issue reports four incidents in an article entitled "Rights Office Investigators Discover It Can Be a Weird World Out There."

The first story is about several administrators at Southern University being charged by a male student with sexual harassment. When asked to be specific, "the student said one official talking to him about a project had told him to 'stay on top of it because some students fall through the cracks.' . . . The student could not name anything that another supposed harasser had done, but said, 'God had given him a vision' that the administrator was harassing him" (*Chronicle*, 21 April 1993).

The second story from the "World of the Weird" is from Penn State's Mont Alto campus. A Hispanic student's parents reportedly requested that their son be allowed to switch dorm rooms because "they didn't want their son living with a black roommate." The university refused, and the student charged the university with "racial discrimination." I guess the question is which student's rights were violated, the Hispanic or the black. Can you figure it out?

The third story involves a student who had left Smith College then applied for readmission. The following statement reportedly appeared on the student's application. "I shall be continue to be [*sic*] peaceful, loving, and will strive for unity but should ANYONE, REPEAT, ANYONE strike me on the left cheek, I shall remove the offending right limb at the shoulder." When Smith College denied the student's application, the student "complained of discrimination."

The final story from the "World of the Weird" occurred at Mississippi State University. A white graduate student charged "that the institution had taken away his teaching assistantship because he was dating a black woman." It turns out that, in fact, "a fellow graduate student, who shared an office with the person bringing the complaint, had arrived one day to find 'the complainant alone, engaging in a sexual act.' " The complainant was then fired for "conduct unbecoming a faculty member."

Before you laugh too loudly at these stories, you should know that each of these complaints was investigated by the Office of Civil Rights *at your expense!* Now, you can laugh. Unfortunately, there's more.

The *Chronicle of Higher Education* reported in its 10 November 1993 issue that members of the University of California at Riverside's chapter of Phi Kappa Sigma fraternity will be required to "undergo sensitivity training" by attending "multicultural-awareness sessions." It seems that in the fall of 1993, members of the fraternity wore T-shirts during rush week which "depicted two Mexicans drinking liquor." When Hispanic students complained, "in effect, the university barred Phi Kappa Sigma from participating in campus activities for at least three years." The Individual Rights Foundation, a public-interest law firm in Los Angeles, filed suit on behalf of the fraternity against the university "under a new state law prohibiting colleges from making or enforcing student-conduct rules that violate free-speech rights." While the court "rescind[ed] the university's penalties," it "enforce[d] other penalties levied by the chapter's parent fraternity, which include attending multicultural sessions" (p. A-32).

Now, if this ruling strikes you as contradictory, you are not alone. The court decided, on the one hand, that penalizing the fraternity members violated their "free-speech rights," and, on the other, allowed the fraternity members to be penalized by being required to attend "multicultural-awareness sessions." Such is the nature of PC antilogic, and, unfortunately, there's still more.

The 1 December 1993 issue of the *Chronicle* reported that in the fall of 1993 at Oberlin College, "someone painted 'dead chink—good chink' and other anti-Asian graffiti on the campus memorial to Christian missionaries killed in China's Boxer Rebellion" (p. A-38). There were two other incidents in the same week (see chapter 4) that made it "seem as if racial and ethnic war were breaking out at Oberlin." Rallies were held on the campus where demands were made for "a tougher hate-crimes code" and for "Oberlin [to] expand its office of minority affairs." But, what appeared to be another example of white racism directed against an ethnic minority turned out to be something very different, indeed.

It was reported that, after the rallies and the protests and the angry demands, "in a letter to the campus newspaper and in an interview with the paper, a student identified only as an Asian claimed responsibility for the graffiti on the Memorial Arch." The student reportedly said that the purpose was "to make the point that the arch 'glorifies white accomplishment' because it doesn't mention the Chinese who died in the Boxer Rebellion." So, again, what appeared to be an example of Eurocentric, white racism directed against a minority, in fact turned out to be nothing of the kind.

The strangest aspect of this story, however, is that "Diem Nguyen, co-chairwoman of the Asian-American Alliance, referring to the arch incident [said], 'Whatever the color or race of the student, it was a racist attack.' " I would agree and I would submit that whites deserve an apology for the knee-jerk responses of those who made the assumption on the basis of PC stereotypes that such an incident could only be perpetrated by whites. I *would* agree, if that were the point that Ms. Nguyen was trying to make, but it appears that's not what she meant at all.

A meeting was organized by "student leaders" to discuss possible responses to the "incidents" at Oberlin, but the meeting was "restricted to 'people of color.' " When a white student showed up and refused to leave, he reportedly "was dragged out by a black senior, Myron Ruffin, and a black visiting professor of sculpture, John Coleman." Ms. Nguyen's response was, "He [the white student who 'was dragged out' of the meeting] was excluded for one hour of one day, but we are excluded for the whole four years we are here." Now doesn't that sound sensitive.

If Ms. Nguyen's comment is not incredible enough, the *Chronicle* also reported that "both the student and professor [who dragged the white student out of the meeting] may face disciplinary action." *May* face disciplinary action? *May?* That means there's a possibility that they *won't* face disciplinary action? I wonder what would have happened if a black student or a Hispanic student or an Asian student would have been dragged out of a meeting restricted to whites only.

There will be more on this very disturbing incident in the next chapter. For the time being, suffice it to say that this is yet another example of the gross, naked hypocrisy so rampant not only in this multicultural business, but in the entire politically correct movement.

Before you dismiss the preceding stories as silly extremism or isolated anecdotes and not really indicative of the power of the politically correct push toward multicultural goals, please know that not only has this virus reached epidemic proportions on our campuses here and in other countries as well, this infection has also found its way off campus and into the general population. As Frederick Crews, chairman of the English department at the University of California at Berkeley, pointed out in an article in the *Chronicle of Higher Education*, "in the 1980s, post-structuralism [the linguistic base of multiculturalism] formed a green-card marriage with the American left. It latched onto a political content and lingo" (13 October 1993, p. A-9).

There are, for example, provinces in Canada that have already mandated by law that half of the seats in the legislature *must* be held by women, and there are congressional districts being drawn in the United States to "assure the election of blacks" to Congress. I am all too familiar with this politically correct game because one of the congressional districts that has been affected by it is mine, the one in which I was a candidate for the U. S. Congress on two separate occasions. The fact that drawing district lines in this manner not only dilutes black political strength but is also blatant gerrymandering, which is expressly illegal, does not seem to matter at all.

Now, in this climate, is it really all that farfetched to imagine Act-Up! and Queer Nation demanding a congressional district for gays and lesbians. Don't dismiss such a notion too lightly until you read chapter 6 of this book, "The Gay Nineties: Beyond Tolerance." The point is that to do what we have done in the name of multiculturalism is to place your foot on a very slippery slope, and at the bottom of that slope is a PC Never-Never Land with dizzying rides that numb the brain and render one incapable of rational thought.

The fact also remains that all this would be laughable if it were not so serious in its consequences. As Heather MacDonald suggested in her *Wall Street Journal* piece referred to earlier in this chapter, all this "obsessive emphasis" on multiculturalism and/or diversity and/or difference is dividing American society and culture against itself, and it must be rejected. It is one thing to be "tolerant." It is one thing to be willing to look to other cultures to see what they might have to offer in terms of insights into the human condition. It is one thing to be aware of one's cultural and ethnic heritage and even to celebrate that heritage. It is quite another thing to elevate race, ethnicity, and culture to the level of a religion and then to maintain that all these things are equal. As Don Feder pointed out in his book, *A Jewish Conservative Looks at Pagan America* (Huntington House Publishers, 1993),

> I do not for a minute believe that mandarin society, which crippled women by binding their feet, or Indian society, which burned widows on their husband's funeral pyres, and Aztec society, which sacrificed virgins by the tens of thousands, are the equivalent of a culture that invented the concept of individual rights, launched the industrial revolution, and doubled the human life span within two centuries.

Well said, sir. Well said.

We must remember that America also has a culture that is unique, and we are all a part of that culture. The cultural heritage we share as Americans, while not perfect, is still, as Mr. Feder so eloquently states, the best that has been achieved so far. Let us work together to make our culture, American culture, better. Let us also denounce those who condemn it and are now seeking to "redefine" it out of existence. In America, the land of *e pluribus unum*, we have sacrificed our *unum* on the altar of our *pluribus*, and it would behoove us to remember the biblical warning that "a house divided against itself *cannot* stand."

While we're on this subject, I would share with you a final, interesting "anecdote" involving Al Gore and our country's motto. According to the 10 January 1994 issue of the *Washington Post* in a section entitled "In the Loop," while speaking to the Institute of World Affairs in Milwaukee and "extolling America's legacy of tolerance among ethnic groups—a tolerance in short supply these days around the globe, Gore said Milwaukee's ethnic melting pot shows that America 'can be *e pluribus unum*—out of one, many.' " No kidding, Gore *really* said that.

Now, for those of you whose Latin is rusty, Gore got it backward. As the *Washington Post* article, which is entitled "For Gore, It's All in the Translation," points out, the slogan "Out of one, many" was the motto of the Soviet Union. *Our* motto, *America's* motto is, "Out of many, one." However, given the profoundly relative, politically correct, postmodern philosophy, words can mean whatever we want them to mean anyway, so I guess it really doesn't matter that Gore literally turned the motto of America inside out by getting the translation exactly wrong. The politically correct, poststructural, deconstructive question would be, "Wrong according to whom?" Or is that, according to who? Oh well, I guess that doesn't matter either.

Perhaps more to the point is that, given the climate today and the apparent growing fragmentation and Balkanization of our society with all the "obsessive emphasis" on difference and diversity and multiculturalism, Gore's mistranslation seems strangely appropriate. But, certainly, the Clinton administration is not committed to reversing America's motto and hopelessly dividing our society along racial, ethnic, and gender lines, right? So Gore's gaffe must have been a mistake, right? Sure. Still, one cannot help but wonder how this incident would have been covered by the mainstream media and treated by the entertainment industry if Dan Quayle had made the comment.

Chapter Four

———————————— ✧ ————————————

Afrocentrism:
Beyond Civil Rights

I mentioned in my introduction that although the politically correct phenomenon has much in common with sixties activism, it also in many ways contradicts the spirit of that time, and it is my view that the most glaring of those contradictions is in the area of race relations. During the sixties, as I recall, real efforts were made to erase color lines. In fact, that was the very essence of the civil rights movement and the heart of the message of Dr. Martin Luther King, Jr. I was inspired by Dr. King and his message, which, to me, was a clarion call to *all* of us to be more than we ever thought we could be, to rise above petty differences and ascend together to that high place, that spiritual plateau where we could celebrate our common humanity. And, oh yes, he spoke often about God and about how truly great the *idea* of America was.

It is very revealing that Dr. King's status as *the* icon of black pride and achievement seems to have diminished to be replaced by the new mystique of Malcolm X. Again, as I recall, and I was alive at the time, there were profound differences between these two men and their messages, and those differences provide significant insight into how far away from the spirit of the sixties, which inspired me, the politically correct phenomenon has moved. I would also point to the recent "treatment" of Malcolm X as an example of the historical revisionism so characteristic of the politically correct phenomenon. Again, I was alive at the time, and I saw Malcolm X on television and read about him, and I remember his message to be a frightening one. But, even if Malcolm X did experience an epiphany and did, in fact, abandon his message of achieving social change through violence (as the politically correct entertainment industry would have us believe), there can be no denying that the color lines that so many worked so hard to erase during the sixties are being redrawn even more stringently than before the civil rights movement began. The irony is that, this time, it is blacks more than any other group who are drawing those lines.

As I stated in my first book on this subject, Afrocentrism is a specialized area of PC multiculturalism featuring the group that has come to call itself "African-Americans." Like all other aspects of the politically correct movement, Afrocentrism has an agenda that, according to the 23 September 1991 issue of *Newsweek* magazine, is "to assert the primacy of traditional African civilizations." According to Afrocentric scholars, "European civilization was derived from Africa [specifically Egypt]," and "the intellectual history of the West [is] a frantic effort to deny this truth" (*Newsweek*, pp. 44–45). Pulitzer Prize winning historian Arthur Schlesinger maintains that what Afrocentric scholars are "saying, essentially, is that Africa is the source of all good and Europe is the source of all evil" (*Newsweek*, p. 42). Lynne Cheny, former chair of the National Endowment for the Humanities, agrees and says, "There seems to be a central theme that anything that happens in the West is bad and everything out of Africa is good" (*Newsweek*, p. 46).

Not only is this "assert[ing] the primacy of traditional African civilizations" through Egypt based on faulty premises, as I discussed at length in my first book on this subject, but the revision of history, which involves distortion of historical fact and even geographical fact, is perhaps nowhere more apparent than in this particular manifestation of the politically correct phenomenon.

Cain Hope Felder, a professor at Howard University's Divinity School, for instance,

> says the image of a white Jesus is one symbol of a "vast complex system of Eurocentrism that permeates the entire academic curriculum." . . . Mr. Felder, who is an ordained Methodist minister, describes Jesus as a "person of color," adding: "If he lived today, here in Washington, he would be a soul brother."

Professor Felder claims to be "waging an 'intellectual war' to show how white biblical scholars have ignored the importance of Africa and its people," and he concludes that "Jesus was definitively black" (*Chronicle of Higher Education*, 16 June 1993, p. A-7).

As with all other facets of the politically correct phenomenon, this concept has found its way off campus through both the mainstream media and the entertainment industry. For example, the sitcom "Martin" did a Christmas episode that featured a black Mary and Joseph. By the way, according to this show, it was because they were black that they were turned away from the inn. This a clear example of sophistic distortion of historical fact for the sake of a political agenda. Based on this kind of thinking, one could and perhaps should question the "whiteness of Santa Claus." Because Santa Claus is a cultural symbol of generosity, the reasoning would be, his "whiteness" could send the wrong signal to black kids. Given the climate, is such a position so far-fetched?

Speaking of far-fetched, as an example of where PC lines converge, I would point to the black minister who had distributed condoms in his church, which I discussed in my first book on this subject. Appearing on a *Donahue* program, this minister stated, "If Jesus were here today, he'd say to Mary [Magdeline], 'Now, Mary, you gotta stop

this, but I know how you are, so, just in case, use this,'
and he'd give her a condom." If I had not heard this with
my own ears, I wouldn't believe it. Talk about revisionism. Talk about missing the point. But, of course, in the
era of politically correct deconstruction and sophistry,
one can interpret any piece of writing in any way he/she
feels is appropriate. Where will it end?

Two other historical personages who were black according to Afrocentric scholars, as I mentioned in my
first book on this subject, include Beethoven and Robert
Browning. As if that list is not bad enough, it continues
to grow. More recently, during a discussion in a modern
fiction class I was teaching, one of my students insisted
that William Faulkner was black. At an academic conference in Dallas where I was the keynote speaker, I told that
story about Faulkner being black during my address.
Afterward, a professor of history from Texas A & M came
over and told me that he had a student in one of his
classes who had recently insisted that Eli Whitney was
black.

An article in *Newsweek* proclaimed in its subtitle, "The
newest icon of multiculturalism is . . . Huck Finn? It could
only happen in academia" (20 July 1992, p. 64). Shelly
Fisher Fishkin, a professor at the University of Texas,
published a book recently entitled *Was Huck Black?* In this
book, Fishkin takes the position that "a black child rather
than a white one . . . [was] the model for the voice with
which Twain would change the shape of American Literature." The fact that Mark Twain made it clear that "Huck
was an exact portrait of a boyhood chum named Tom
Blankenship, the son of the town drunk in Hannibal,
Missouri" doesn't seem to matter. Still, such politically
correct claims must be treated with respect. So even though
Pulitzer Prize-winning Twain biographer Justin Kaplan
"was one of the few to betray discomfort with the slender-
ness of Fishkin's evidence, [he still] gave her an A for
effort. 'I wish there'd been more proof,' [Kaplan said]"
(*Newsweek*, 20 July 1992, p. 64). Fishkin's claim is that
Huck was based on a "little darkey boy" whom Twain met

in 1871 or 1872 and whom he nicknamed "Sociable Jimmy" in a *New York Times* piece. The *Newsweek* article concludes by admitting that although "no one can prove Twain *didn't* get [Huck] from Sociable Jimmy . . . Fishkin hasn't proved he did" (p. 65). Unfortunately, that's what scholars are *supposed* to do, and simply asserting something that no one can disprove does not make it so, unless, of course, we're playing PC sophistry.

Syndicated columnist Don Feder reported in *A Jewish Conservative Looks at Pagan America* (Huntington House Publishers, 1993) that he encountered a "prominent Mad Hatter from multicultural land" who asked him did he "know there were Jews in Columbus' crew." When Feder replied that he had "heard there were Marranos (Jews forced to convert during the Inquisition) on the venerable voyage," his inquisitor said, "No, no, these were *Moorish* (black) Jews." The person then asked Feder if he were "further apprised that the 'original Jews' were black." Feder, thinking he had "misunderstood" the man, said that he "knew there were black Jews from Ethiopia. . . . But surely he wasn't suggesting that Abraham, Isaac, and Jacob were black?" To Feder's dismay, "That was precisely his point."

This kind of nonsense has even drawn criticism from prominent black scholars. For instance, Frank Snowden of Howard University, "arguably America's greatest black classicist," said, "Many students have already been misled and confused by Afrocentrists' inaccuracies and omissions in their treatment of blacks in the ancient Mediterranean world. The time has come for Afrocentrists to cease mythologizing and falsifying the past" (*Measure*, January 1992, No. 102, p. 10).

For examples of just how "misled and confused" some students have been by Afrocentric claims, I needed to look no further than the *Vermilion*, the student newspaper on my own campus. The 31 January 1992 issue contained a piece entitled "Schools Choose to Eliminate Important Historical Records." The author of this piece, a young black female and a former student of mine, admits that she "did not even know that Egypt was a part of Africa" and uses this as proof of a conscious conspiracy propagated through the U.S. educational system to intentionally keep black students ignorant of the "real" history of Africa and the West. After citing several, at best, questionable "facts," the writer ends by asserting,

> I have come to the belief that history in the school system sometimes chooses to eliminate important records and documents of past events. I have come to believe that since the trans-Atlantic slave trade, history has been used didactically to keep an oppressed people neglected of their history, thus making it harder for them to deal with their own present.

Another editorial, which appeared in the 8 November 1991 issue of the *Vermilion*, goes even further. Consider the following excerpts.

> Today, African-Americans are still faced with slavery—MENTAL SLAVERY. . . . The American system, which was created out of the racist ideology of Europeans, further developed the mental slavery among African-Americans and continues to do so today. . . .

> One of the key elements Europeans used to contribute to the slave mentalities of African-Americans was religion. Presently, European religion, "Christianity," remains the key element keeping African-American minds in bondage. . . .

> History documents that the teachings of the Bible and Christianity are actually derived from the writings of ancient African priests, rulers, and philosophers. Ancient African texts document the first stories of the Annunciation, the Immaculate Conception, the Virgin Birth and the world's first Savior, who was proclaimed as the Son of God. All of the documents were written over 4,000 years before the birth of the Christian Son of God, "Jesus the Christ."

> . . . African-Americans, and many others who call themselves "Christians," must realize that their religion is nothing more than a European version of African philosophy and religious thought.

As Dr. Gary Marotta, academic vice-president of my university who also holds a Ph.D. in history, pointed out, not only is this piece historically inaccurate, it is a contradiction in terms. Henry Louis Gates, Jr., director of Harvard's African-American studies program and arguably the most distinguished black scholar in the world, also points to the irony of Afrocentric scholars and their progeny vilifying and condemning Western culture as racist then going to such great lengths "to claim authorship" of all its achievements and traditions. Yet, such logically contradictory and historically inaccurate "notions" are continuing to be asserted as matters of fact, and this is typical of politically correct thinking, which bears a striking resemblance to what Plato called the "antilogic" of the Sophists (see chapter 2). When the political agenda is paramount, then one does not need to worry about accuracy, evidence, or consistency. But, perhaps even more troubling than the distortion of history upon which so much of Afrocentrism seems to rest is the effect that it has had of producing a group of people who seem bound and determined to see virtually everything they behold as an example of racism.

As I mentioned in my introduction, "The colors of the tassels on graduates' mortarboards has become an issue at Camden County College." The position has been taken by black students in letters to the student newspaper that the fact that the tassels are black is "a racial issue. . . . 'Black does not need to represent the lowest,' wrote one" (*Chronicle of Higher Education*, 15 December 1993, p. A-5).

As I also mentioned in chapter 3, black students on my campus objected to our school's sports mascot, the Ragin' Cajun. When the story appeared in the student newspaper, it was reported that one of the bases for the objection was that the word "Ragin" spelled backward is a racial slur. Our mascot is no longer the Ragin' Cajun. It is now a bulldog, but we still call the teams the Cajuns. You figure it out.

It remains a question in my mind as to just what is more amazing, the fact that some people continue to come up with such "issues" or the fact that we discuss them seriously. Regardless, it is as amazing as it is discouraging that such "issues" seem to be occupying more and more of our time and energy these days. I suppose the moral to these and so many other stories like them is that if you look hard enough, eventually, you will find what you're looking for. Again, it seems that the PC crowd is capable of seeing racism in virtually everything, from the tassels on graduate mortarboards to calls for higher academic standards.

The accusation has actually been made that those of us who have been and continue to call for more stringent academic standards in our educational system are racists and that our demand for higher standards is nothing more than a "covert racist agenda." The media attention to this debate has been focused on athletics. What sparked the ongoing controversy was when the NCAA attempted to impose minimum academic standards for incoming freshman athletes through its Proposition 48. John Thompson, the basketball coach at Georgetown, walked off the floor during a game to protest the move which, according to Thompson, was racist.

As reported in 20 October 1993 issue of the *Chronicle of Higher Education*, when about three hundred and fifty members of the National Association of Basketball Coaches met in Charlotte, North Carolina, in the fall of 1993 "to discuss subjects ranging from ethics to National Collegiate Athletic Association rules that govern their sport . . . the black coaches . . . [were] particularly upset about the NCAA's tougher academic standards, set to take effect in 1995" (p. A-54). It was also reported that "opponents of such standards [minimum academic standards] object to the use of standardized-test scores as absolute cutoffs for eligibility because they say the tests are culturally biased and thus unfairly shut out many black athletes" (*Chronicle*, 5 January 1994, p. A-47).

Attacking the validity of "standardized" tests like the SAT and the ACT, which colleges and universities use in various ways to admit and/or place incoming students, is a very common PC tactic. The PC crowd argues that such tests can never effectively measure a student's potential. The appropriate response is that is *not* what we're trying to measure. These tests are designed to give us some idea of what our students *know*, not what they might one day be. In addition, the folks who claim the tests are "culturally biased" obviously maintain that they are biased toward middle and upper middle class white kids. This position is based upon the statistical analyses that show that black kids do not do as well on these tests as white kids.

The problem with this position is that the ethnic group that performs *best* on these tests are Asians. Now a rational, reasonable person would conclude that, given the performance of Asian-American kids, many of whom are first generation immigrants, the position that the tests are "culturally biased" simply doesn't hold up. A rational, reasonable person might also be inclined to ask just what we are supposed to use if we throw out "standardized" tests? Pulse rates? Blood pressure? Eye exams? But, the beauty of PC antilogic is, again, that the political agenda supersedes all other considerations so you don't have to let rational analysis or reasonable questions stand in your way. And, as always, just when you think things are really strange, they get worse.

The latest development in this ongoing debate of imposing "tougher academic standards" is that a member of Congress has weighed in. Congresswoman Cardiss L. Collins, a Democrat from Illinois, and the Black Coaches Association, a national organization of high-school and college coaches, "called for an investigation of NCAA researchers and for postponement of the athletic association's plan to raise academic-eligibility standards" (*Chronicle*, 5 January 1994, p. A-47). Representative Collins and the black coaches "have charged that researchers hired by the NCAA to analyze data on academic standards for athletes have links to a group that espouses genetic engineering." Those making the allegations are attempting to establish links between three members of the data-analysis group retained by the NCAA and a man by the name of Raymond B. Cattell, the founder of the movement called "Beyondism," which "favors such policies as eugenics, or hereditary improvement by selective breeding."

The "links" that Congresswoman Collins and the Black Coaches Association allege are, at best, tenuous, at least according to the information contained in the *Chronicle* article. Nevertheless, even if evidence is forthcoming which strengthens those "links," basing the conclusion that the NCAA, and all other educators calling for stricter academic standards, are really just executing a covert racist agenda still seems to involve a huge leap in logic. As Alan Kraut, executive director of the American Psychological Society pointed out,

> These guilt-by-association charges are not only wrong, but dangerous. Cattell is a pioneer in this special area, and you can't be an expert in multivariant experimental analysis without having read and seriously studied Cattell's work in the mathematical discipline. That work, for most researchers, has nothing to do with Cattell's other ideas. (*Chronicle*, p. A-47)

Still, Congresswoman Collins and the Black Coaches Association have ignored the calm and compelling argument of Mr. Kraut, as well as the other rational problems, with objecting to using standardized tests and boldly leap the logical chasm to land softly at the mind-boggling position that we are about to see a reenactment of the Holocaust! Rudy Washington, executive director of the Black Coaches Association, issued this statement: "Fifty years ago, millions of Jews were herded onto railroad cars and sent to their deaths. Letting this group continue to advise the NCAA can only propagate the same basic ideas of a superior race. We *must* protect our children from the same fate" (*Chronicle*, p. A-47).

Now this is good even for PC antilogic. The always veiled suggestion that there is actually a connection between the NCAA and other educators calling for higher academic standards and the Nazis has finally been stated outright. Another example of this "connection" being stated rather than merely suggested is found in the statements of Alvin O. Chambliss, Jr., a civil rights lawyer who was actually quoted in the 17 November 1993 issue of the *Chronicle of Higher Education* as saying that "raising [academic] standards . . . was a 'racist ploy' to limit black students' ability to go to college" (p. A-31). Clearly, this is evidence of the fact that this accusation is not being levelled only at the NCAA but at *all* of us who insist that higher standards are necessary. At least now those of us who really do believe that our educational system needs to establish clear and stringent academic standards can discuss this accusation in a more straightforward manner because the "connection" between us and the Nazis is no longer just cleverly implied but clearly stated.

If you think about it, whenever the charge of "racism" is levelled at someone, that person stands accused of Nazi-like attitudes because, in the hierarchy of racists, I assume that most people would agree that the Nazis occupy the most prominent position. So, maybe the link between imposing higher academic standards on students and "herd[ing] Jews onto railroad cars and [sending] them to their deaths" isn't that big a leap for PC antilogic after all. Nevertheless, that is clearly what Mr. Washington has done in his "statement," and, while his "statement" may make sense in the world of PC sophistry, it strikes me as unbelievably hysterical to suggest that he and his colleagues "*must* protect [their] children from the same fate" suffered by the Jews during World War II. I also find his position deeply offensive and an affront not only to intellectual honesty but to basic decency.

These stories, and there are so many of them, reveal the reason that the politically correct movement has been

compared to the McCarthyism of the fifties. The PC crowd
appears absolutely intent on finding a homophobe in
every closet, a sexist under every bed, and a racist behind
every tree. The mouths of the PCers are like semiauto-
matic weapons when it comes to hurling these vicious
epithets revealing both the penchant for *ad hominem* attack as well as just how mindless so much of the politically
correct phenomenon has become. In fact, the PC crowd's
careless and constant use of labels like racist has not only
damaged their credibility by likening them to "the boy
who cried wolf," it also seems to have removed the real
force from these labels. In addition, as is normally the
case with manifestations of PC antilogic, a glaring hypocrisy is involved. Consider the following "anecdotes."

In the 13 October 1993 issue of the *Chronicle of Higher
Education*, it was reported that nine nooses were found
hanging from trees around the campus of Ithaca College
in Ithaca, New York. Also found near the nooses were
"wooden plates" with "the names of well-known African-
Americans" written on them. The *Chronicle* article specifically mentioned the names of Lani Guinier and Malcolm X.

Administrators at Ithaca College, "fear[ing] the display was an attempt at intimidation by white racists . . .
ordered the nooses taken down" and "issued a statement
that said, 'Neither racism nor threats of any kind will be
tolerated' " (p. A-2). Now, at first glance, the administration's
response would appear to be reasonable because, surely,
this "display" had to be the work of right-wing, neo-Nazi,
skinheaded, fundamentalist Christian, College Republicans. *Not!*

It turns out that the organizer of the "display" was
black! The black student, Justin M. Chapman, who admitted placing the nooses and wooden plates around the
campus, "said the display was a conceptual-art project
designed 'to provoke reaction, thought, and discussions
on race-related issues.' " I leave it to you, my thoughtful
readers, to reflect on the consequences this student would
have faced if he had been white.

The *Chronicle of Higher Education* also reported in the

1 December 1991 issue that "for about a week this fall, it seemed as if racial and ethnic war were breaking out at Oberlin College" (p. A-38). Several "incidents" that appeared to be racial in nature occurred on the campus, not the least of which was the discovery of burning crosses outside a residence hall. These events, which clearly had to be the work of right-wing, neo-Nazi, skin-headed, conservative, Christian College Republicans, were denounced at rallies where shrill cries for "a tougher hate-crimes code" and stern demands that "Oberlin expand its office of minority affairs" were heard.

> It turned out, however, that not all was what it seemed. Students who live in the residence hall where the crosses were found came forward . . . to confess that what seemed racist was really a Halloween prank. The students said they had burned scarecrows, and the smoldering remains looked like crosses. (*Chronicle*, p. A-38)

Now, it seems to me that a rational, reasonable response to this sequence of events would be for everyone to *think* more carefully about what racism *really* is. Alas, another troubling characteristic of PC thinkers is that they seem incapable of admitting when they are wrong, as they clearly were in the incident at Oberlin. Rather than realizing that they really should slow down those PC rapid-fire responses and knee-jerk tendencies to see racism, sexism, and homophobia in even the most innocuous of places and contemplate the theme developed in literature for centuries that things are not always what they appear to be, students at Oberlin "say the Halloween pranksters showed stunning insensitivity in allowing even the appearance of burning crosses." Now *that's* PC logic, but stay tuned; it gets worse.

Another meeting was held on the campus "to talk about possible responses to the incidents," but attendance was limited to "people of color." During the meeting, a white student who refused to leave was dragged out by a black senior, Myron Ruffin, and a black visiting professor of sculpture, John Coleman. Now, please understand that, according to the *Chronicle of Higher Education*, a *faculty* member physically removed a student from a meeting on campus to discuss racism, simply because he was white. But, it gets even worse. "Later that night, the white student, Chapin Benninghoff, found a garbage can on fire outside his door, and the words 'Racists must die' painted on a nearby wall." This is all in response to what *appeared* to be a racist statement that turned out to be nothing but the remnants of a Halloween party.

Now, it would appear that the *real* racism is to be found in the *response*, which certainly *appears* to be out of all proportion to the original incident. But, if you find my analysis of this strange tale reasonable and logical, then you're a racist because, according to PC antilogic, black people *cannot* be racists. I have heard it said again and again that you can't be a racist if you don't have power, and, since blacks have no power, they can't be racists. Even though a white student was physically removed from a meeting on his campus by a black faculty member and a black student, the blacks who did the "removing" cannot be racists because they have no power. Now, if this position is logical, then I have no concept of what logic is because, to my politically incorrect way of thinking, this violates all categories of rational thought. Not only does this "anecdote" stand as an example of the nature of PC antilogic, it is further evidence of the hypocrisy of it as well. While vociferously condemning racism and seeing it in the most innocuous of places, the PC crowd is incapable of recognizing it in all circumstances, in the existence of "black" colleges, for instance.

First of all, a rational, reasonable person might be inclined to ask how we could even have such a thing as "black" colleges in this country. After all, didn't *Brown v. Board of Education* make racially segregated institutions unconstitutional? One would have thought so, but, according to the *Chronicle of Higher Education's* 1 December 1993 issue, there are 117 "traditionally black colleges and universities" (p. A-30). And, not only do "black" colleges exist, they're a big budget item.

> A federal capital fund created by Congress during the 1992 reauthorization of the Higher Education Act is intended to make possible some . . . [construction] projects at . . . historically black colleges and universities. The [federal] government will make available to those colleges up to $357 million in loans at below market rates. (*Chronicle*, p. A-30)

A reasonable, rational person might be inclined to point out that $357 million is really not that much money considering the size of the federal budget, a point that I would readily concede. I would also point out, however, that as a wise member of Congress once said, "A million here and a million there and pretty soon you're talking real money." Furthermore, the money is not even the issue. The issue is whether "traditionally black colleges and universities" are constitutional given *Brown v. Board of Education*, and the point is what would happen if we referred to *any* institution in this country as a "traditionally white college or university"? I suggest that the answer is not only obvious, that answer is, as I maintained earlier, yet another example of the glaring hypocrisy of PC sophistry.

For yet another example of a glaring inconsistency that reveals the deep-seated hypocrisy of the whole PC phenomenon, consider this. When questions are raised as to the legitimacy and constitutionality of "traditionally black colleges and universities," the voices that protest loudest are those of *blacks*. But, how can this be, a reasonable, rational person might ask, when, as I mentioned earlier, the primary focus of the original civil rights movement was desegregation, and specifically, desegregation of *schools*. The troubling answer, which seems to be becoming clearer all the time, is that blacks want it both ways. Today, desegregation means integration of "white" institutions while "traditionally black" ones can not only be preserved, new ones (like the *Black* Miss America Pageant) can be created. And, if you dare to question this, you're a racist.

According to the *Chronicle of Higher Education*, "The U.S. Supreme Court ruled in 1992 that vestiges of segregation remained in Mississippi's college system" (17 November 1993, p. A-31). W. Ray Clere, Mississippi's higher education commissioner and the chief staff person to the Board of Trustees of Institutions of Higher Learning, who calls himself "a leftover advocate of the absolute integration of higher education in America," attempted to obey the law and honor the court's ruling and do something about the "vestiges of segregation [which] remained in Mississippi's college system." Mr. Clere said, "I do not believe the answer lies in continuing the identifiability of white and black institutions in terms of their racial heritage" (p. A-32). Still, Clere's efforts to desegregate Mississippi's institutions of higher learning drew sharp criticism. And, the strongest criticism he drew was from, you guessed it, African-Americans. In other words, today we have blacks defending public institutions that are *de facto* segregated and a clear violation of *Brown v. Board of Education*, so long as they are black institutions.

We have a similar situation here in Louisiana. There are two predominantly black public universities that would appear to be in clear violation of *Brown v. Board of Education*. In fact, a federal court so ruled over twenty years ago, and we have been operating under a so-called Consent Decree since that time. Every time a plan is submitted that is supposedly an attempt to comply with the twenty-year old federal court order, blacks insist that the "integrity" of the predominantly black institutions be preserved. But, the integrity of the predominantly black institutions is the reason we are in violation of *Brown v. Board of Education* and are under a federal "Consent Decree" in the first place. Still, the state of Louisiana continues to maintain two separate university systems, one predominantly white and one predominantly black, and the predominantly white one is much more integrated than the predominantly black one. The only "good" thing that has come from this is that the endless litigation has kept quite a few lawyers in business.

An interesting twist to the story of these "traditionally black colleges and universities" is the increasing number of complaints and lawsuits being filed against them on the basis of racial discrimination. A headline in the 21 April 1993 issue of the *Chronicle of Higher Education* reads, "White Professor Wins Discrimination Suit Against Black College." According to the story, Allan D. Cooper sued St. Augustine College in June of 1992, alleging that he had been denied tenure because he is white. According to Cooper, "the college awarded tenure to three black professors, none of whom had been formally reviewed for tenure." Cooper also maintained that "his credentials were stronger than all three professors." In fact, "with three books and 25 articles to his credit, he had the strongest record of scholarship in the college" (p. A-17). On the "issue of tenure," Mr. Cooper claimed that there was "a glass ceiling." "As a white professor," he said, "you could be welcomed in any other aspect of college life, but the administration didn't want to make the relationship permanent. . . . Unfortunately . . . what we're seeing . . . is that there are some African-Americans who use power the same way whites do" (*Chronicle*, 13 October 1993, p. A-20). Imagine that.

Now, if the court defined *racism* the way the PC crowd does, it would have to have thrown out Mr. Cooper's suit because black people can't be racist and, therefore, one would presume, could not be guilty of racial discrimination. But, the court did not rule on the basis of the PC definition of racism. It awarded Cooper $745,000. There's another twist, however. "Although gratified by his court victory, Mr. Cooper said he expected nonetheless to be out of a job in May [of 1993]. . . . He said, 'the bottom line is, I didn't get tenure' " (*Chronicle*, 21 April 1993, p. A-17).

The 13 October 1993 issue of the *Chronicle* reports several cases of alleged discrimination by black colleges against white professors. "Three white professors of law have sued Texas Southern University, claiming that they are paid $4,000 to $5,000 less than their black colleagues with similar experience" (p. A-20).

In addition, "white members of the nursing faculty have accused Grambling State of race discrimination, and all three have filed complaints with the EEOC (Equal Employment Opportunity Commission)." They charge that "a black professor received a $7,000 raise, while white professors with more experience got nothing" and "that newly recruited black faculty members were offered much higher salaries than white professors who had been on the campus for years and had more experience" (p. A-20).

Complaints have also been filed with EEOC by two faculty members at Elizabeth City State University. Carol S. O'Dell, an associate professor of mathematics, and Carol S. Kerr, an assistant professor of education, have accused the school of "race and sex discrimination." The complaint filed by Professor O'Dell stems from an incident involving the school's chancellor, Jimmy R. Jenkins. In the fall of 1993, O'Dell "publicly accused Mr. Jenkins of racism after he said at a campus meeting that 'white faculty who don't like the way we do things here' should find another job. Mr. Jenkins later apologized but said he was misunderstood" (*Chronicle*, 17 November 1993, p. A-23). Professor O'Dell's response was, "When you're a woman in mathematics, you have spent your life in a minority situation, so this is not new to me. However, such blatant racism as is practiced here [Elizabeth City State University] is. I can't imagine any white chancellor in this country being allowed to make the statement Jenkins did and keep his job" (*Chronicle*, 13 October 1993, p. A-20).

The "blatant racism" of which Professor O'Dell speaks is apparently not just directed at white faculty. A white student at Elizabeth City State University who "asks that her name not be used because she fears retaliation" told the *Chronicle* that "someone in one of her classes put up a sign on the chalkboard that had a circle with the word 'Whites' written in the middle with a slash through it." She added that "she was the only white student in the class" and that "she had previously written an evaluation criticizing the instructor, who was black" (*Chronicle*, 13 October 1993, p. A-22).

The 13 October 1993 issue of the *Chronicle of Higher Education* reported that Billy Foster, a senior at Fayetteville State University, "became the first white student chosen to be a drum major in the campus marching band. In August, he resigned amid pressure from black students outside the band who felt that leadership positions on the campus should be held by black students" (p. A-22). Although it was also reported that Mr. Foster "resumed his post after being encouraged by many black students and the university's chancellor, Lloyd V. Hackley," the fact that the incident occurred at all is yet more evidence of a very troubling trend on campuses across this country.

Samuel DuBois Cook, president of Dillard University, was quoted in that same issue of the *Chronicle* as saying, "In the 1960s, black colleges were under pressure to maintain their identity." He added that he recalled "some black students then calling for the dismissal of all white professors and administrators" (p. A-20). Sadly, it seems that, indeed, the more things change, the more they stay the same, and clearly, like Lewis Carroll's Alice, we have entered some strange parallel, upside down universe where reverse discrimination is the norm, but it is not recognized as such because of the sophistic, politically correct position that blacks can't be racists.

Kan V. Chandras, a professor of education at Fort Valley State College in Fort Valley, Georgia claims to "have been experiencing reverse discrimination for years." It is interesting to note that Mr. Chandras identifies himself as a faculty member "neither white nor black." Professor Chandras maintains that "as president of an American Association of University Professors chapter, [he has] received legitimate reverse-discrimination complaints from white professors and others such as Asian Indians, Koreans, Chinese, and Middle Eastern scholars." His conclusion is unusual in its candor. Mr. Chandras says, "It is public knowledge that the Board of Regents is afraid to take any action against administrators at black colleges. Therefore, blatant reverse discrimination continues" (*Chronicle*, 17 November 1993, p. B-6). This troubling reverse discrimination is not, however, confined to "traditionally black colleges."

In the 1 December 1993 issue of the *Chronicle of Higher Education*, several such incidents were reported at universities that are not "traditionally black institutions." For example, graduate students at the University of California at Berkeley protested "when the sociology department offered a job teaching race relations to Loic Wacquant, a young, highly respected scholar who is white. Students wanted the position to go to a minority candidate." Students and community leaders attempted to prevent Candice L. Goucher, a white associate professor of black studies, from being named as head of the black studies department at Portland State University. "At Weber State University, students objected . . . when a white man was hired to teach a variety of courses, including one on black history" (p. A-19). Vince Nobile, a white professor of history at Chaffey College, "decided to stop teaching his black-history courses in the spring of 1992. He says he did not seem to be able to reach black students in the class and they did not trust him—primarily, he says, because of his race" (p. A-20). Professor Nobile wrote a piece about his experience as a white professor of black history, which appeared in the September 1992 issue of *Perspective*, a newsletter published by the American Historical Association. "In the essay, he described his classroom confrontations with black students. He said they had challenged his ability, as a white man, to teach a course in black history and questioned the textbooks he assigned" (*Chronicle*, p. A-20). Another incident involving a white professor teaching black history is perhaps more compelling than Mr. Nobile's case because while he "decided to stop teaching his black-history courses," this story involves attempts by students to *force* a white professor to stop teaching such classes.

Christie Farnham Pope, an associate professor of history at Iowa State University, "has been teaching black-history courses since 1978, and the fact that she is white was never a serious problem—until now." Since the beginning of the 1993 fall semester, "black students have called her racist and protesters have staged silent sit-ins in her classroom" (*Chronicle*, 1 December 1993, p. A-19). It is also reported that "leaders of the Black Student Alliance are continuing to press for Ms. Pope's removal from the classroom" (p. A-20).

The problems apparently stem from a confrontation Professor Pope had with DeAngelo Moore, a freshman at Iowa State who goes by the name of DeAngelo X. According to Pope, "one of the first questions he [Mr. X] asked in class was, Why is a white woman teaching this?" According to the story in the *Chronicle*, there were "many confrontations" after that with Pope accusing DeAngelo X of "constantly disrupting the class to challenge her" (p. A-20). What follows is the rest of the story as it appeared in the *Chronicle*.

> Things came to a head one day when Mr. Moore called Ms. Pope a racist. She asked him to leave the class. He refused. He held up a newspaper with the words "Black power" written on it. When she ignored him, he walked up to the front of the class and placed the newspaper on the lectern. When he turned to walk out of the class, Ms. Pope says she tossed the newspaper on the floor. Some students say she threw it at Mr. Moore, which she denies. (p. A-20)

Another student at Iowa State who also reportedly got involved in the controversy surrounding Professor Pope is Michael D. Boulden, a master's student in marketing. When Pope said that she does not "teach claims that are not validated by good scholarship" and specifically mentioned "Leonard Jefferies, Jr., and others on 'melanin theory,' which ascribes personality traits to people based on their skin color," Mr. Boulden responded by saying, "Dr. Jefferies is a scholar. His theory is just that—a theory. . . . But she [Professor Pope] dismisses it rather than debates it" (*Chronicle*, p. A-20).

Before I conclude Professor Pope's story, I must take some time to talk about this man Jefferies. Although I spoke of him at length in my first book on this subject, I believe it is important to inform those of my readers who are unfamiliar with him about who this man is and what he has said. Leonard Jefferies is the head of the black studies department at City University of New York. He is constantly quoted speaking of "the long-running conspiracy by Western whites to deny the African contribution to civilization" (*New York Magazine*, 21 January 1991, p. 39). According to Mr. Jefferies, this "conspiracy to oppress blacks stretches from classrooms to the Mafia and Jewish movie producers" (*Newsweek*, 23 September 1991, p. 42). He has also been quoted as saying that "Jews and Italians in Hollywood conspired to denigrate blacks in the movies and that rich Jews played a key role in helping to finance the slave trade" (*Chronicle of Higher Education*, 18 December 1991, p. A-17). Jefferies delivered a speech in July of 1991 at a black arts festival in Albany, New York, during which he referred to one of his colleagues as "the head Jew." During this same speech, Jefferies said, "These white folks, even the good ones, you can't trust" (*Chronicle*, p. A-19).

Some of Jefferies comments are so boorish that I am reluctant to quote them verbatim, but I believe that it is necessary for people to understand just what Afrocentrism is capable of producing, in fact, what it has already produced. Fred Rueckher, a former student of Jefferies at CUNY, claimed that Jefferies "attacked black males for succumbing to the 'white p—y syndrome,' that is, pursuing white women." According to Rueckher, Jefferies also called Diana Ross "an 'international whore' for her association with white men." And, he applauded when the Challenger space shuttle exploded because that "would deter white people from 'spreading their filth throughout the universe' " (*New York Magazine*, 21 January 1991, p. 40).

Jefferies has also constructed an anthropological explanation as to just why whites have oppressed blacks throughout human history. His "theory" is that all human beings are divided into only two categories, "ice people" (whites) and "sun people" (blacks). The descendants of ice people "are materialistic, selfish, and violent, while those descended from sun people are nonviolent, cooperative, and spiritual." Jefferies further maintains that "blacks are biologically superior to whites because they have more melanin, and melanin regulates intellect and health" (*New York Magazine*, 21 January 1991, p. 39).

Now, this is the man whose theories Mr. Boulden criticized Professor Pope for refusing to discuss. Mr. Boulden also called Jefferies a "scholar." Jefferies also refers to himself as "a consummate scholar," but, according to the *Chronicle of Higher Education*, his "scholarship has been practically nonexistent since he completed his dissertation ... in 1972." Even Professor Molefi Assente, chair of the department of African-American studies at Temple University and author of the book *Afrocentricity*, who "defends Mr. Jefferies [admits] it's no secret he [Jefferies] hasn't written any books" (*Chronicle*, 18 December 1991, p. A-19). I have some bad news for Mr. Boulden, Mr. Jefferies, and Mr. Asante. "Writing books" is exactly what "consummate scholars" *do*, and, if you don't do that, you have no right referring to yourself as a scholar.

Furthermore, as I pointed out in my first book on this subject, Mr. Jefferies' attitudes are profoundly racist, and his so-called theories not only have no basis in anything remotely scholarly or scientific, they are dangerous. I think that Robert Hinton, assistant professor of history and African-American studies at Kenyon College in Ohio, answered Mr. Boulden's criticism of Professor Pope quite adequately. I quote from Professor Hinton's comments.

> College faculty and administrators must develop the courage to explain to their students that the curriculum is designed neither to make them feel good about themselves nor to teach them what they think they already know. Michael Boulden ... may think that Leonard Jefferies's "melanin theory" is just another theory that deserves debate, but what about all the other "theories" of racial superiority. Does he want Christie Farnham Pope to discuss these as well?

. . . The fact that he thinks that the melanin content of his skin qualifies him to tell a professor
what to teach is evidence that he is a victim of the
same old romantic essentialism that keeps rising
like a vampire to suck the lifeblood out of African-
American studies. It's time we drove a stake
through that monster's heart. (*Chronicle*, 5 January
1994, p. B-4)

Mr. X, the student involved in the original confrontation, also accuses Professor Pope of "ridiculing his religion" for which he reportedly "threatened a 'jihad' or
Muslim holy war, against Ms. Pope." According to Pope,
"she was discussing the spectrum of views that fall under
the rubric of Afrocentrism. He took offense, she says,
when she referred to a Nation of Islam publication as an
example of 'radical' Afrocentrism" (*Chronicle*, p. A-20). In
order to understand Professor Pope's position, it is necessary to be informed about the Nation of Islam and its
recognized leader, Louis Farrakhan.

The Nation of Islam, estimated to have some ten
thousand members, is a group of black Muslims who have
been gaining recognition and credibility. For example,
"last September the Congressional Black Caucus, headed
by Rep. Kweisi Mfume, established a formal relationship
with the Nation of Islam. The caucus even managed to
obtain federal funding for a Nation of Islam AIDS education program" (*Newsweek*, 14 February 1994, p. 48). Louis
Farrakhan speaks all over the country and is often featured on the major television networks and in other major
media outlets. In fact, Farrakhan appeared on CNN as
recently as February of 1994 "saying that 75 percent of
slaves in the American South were owned by Jews. This
is a lie. (The truth is more like 2 percent.) He apparently
misread his own Nation of Islam book, *The Secret Relationship Between Blacks and Jews*, a pseudoscholarly anti-Semitic
tract that claims that 75 percent of urban Southern Jews
owned slaves, which—even if true—is quite a different point"
(*Newsweek*, p. 48).

The most recent controversy in which the Nation of
Islam finds itself embroiled involves a speech given by

one of its members named Khalid Abdul Muhammad,
identified as "the national spokesman for Louis Farrakhan"
(*Vermilion*, 5 November 1993, p. 5). This man spoke on
my campus in the fall of 1992. The chair of the campus
committee who invited Mr. Muhammad said, "I had a
couple of friends who went [to his talk] last year. . . . they
were very, very very offended, very scared about his
message. After they told me some of the stuff that was
said, I felt really sick inside" (*Vermilion*, p. 5). That was
1992. The *Vermilion*, the student newspaper on my campus, also reported, "About 20 students from the African-
American Culture Committee attended the meeting in a
show of support for Muhammad." Several of these students said that "Muhammad's message was highly inspira-
tional" (p. 5).

Mr. Muhammad also spoke at the University of North
Carolina in the fall of 1992. During his remarks, he called
Socrates "a 'faggot'—a comment received with laughter
and applause by many in the crowd." Reportedly, Mr.
Muhammad "followed this cultural insight [about Socrates]
with streams of invective directed at 'blue-eyed devils' and
'crackers.' 'We are,' he announced, 'tired of blond-haired,
pale-skinned blue-eyed buttermilk complexioned cracker
Christ or peckerwood Jesus' " (*Wall Street Journal*, 29 September 1992, p. A-14).

More recently, Muhammad spoke at Kean College in
New Jersey, and it was reported in the 5 January 1994
issue of the *Chronicle of Higher Education* that over "one
hundred students and community members—most of them
black—attended his speech" (p. A-19). According to the
same issue of the *Chronicle*, the "speech contained passages that many on the campus called racist, anti-Semitic,
sexist, and homophobic" (p. A-19). Muhammad reportedly called Columbia a " 'Jew-niversity' and called for the
killing of all white people in South Africa. . . . Speaking
of the Pope, Mr. Muhammad said, 'Someone should lift
that cracker's skirt so we can see what is really under-
neath it' " (p. A-19). *Newsweek* also reported that
Muhammad called Jews "bloodsuckers" (14 February 1994,
p. 48).

Mr. Muhammad appeared again on my campus recently to help celebrate Black History month. Here are some excerpts from his remarks.

> Let me get this straight before I even get started, *guys*. To the whites who are in the audience, and in particular to our friends from the print and electronic media, buckle your seat belts, *guys*.

> . . . For black history celebration, white people give us one month out of the year—the shortest one they could find—to celebrate our greatness, our glory, our honor and to celebrate our infinite history. With 12 months out of the year we must study their moment in time. We can no longer accept a Black History Day, a Black History Week or a Black History Month, knowing that we are the father and mother of all who walk on this earth.

> . . . The Bible says that Jesus had hair like lamb's wool. I'm talking about nappy hair. . . . I'm talking about a black man. I'm talking about a black savior, a black redeemer, a black son of the living God. Don't bring me no blond-haired, blue-eyed, pale-skinned white Jesus!

> You don't really understand, do you, whites, how racist you really are? . . . You no-good hypocrites! You lying hypocrites! I am a mirror for the whites and an alarm clock to wake the blacks! (*The Vermilion*, 11 March 1994, p. 1-2)

Now, one might ask what gives a Muslim the right to comment on *Christian* tradition. That would seem to violate multicultural premises.

I wish to make it known that my university *paid* this man to speak at my campus, and I assume that he is paid whenever he speaks at universities. I would also point out that, according to the *Vermilion*, not only was the hall in which Mr. Muhammad spoke filled, the overflow was taken to another room where his speech was broadcast on widescreen TVs. After Muhammad's speech, Jalaenda Greene, a freshman in elementary education at Grambling, said, "I thought his message was great. It was very inspiring" (*Vermilion*, 11 March 1994, p. 2). USL student body president Shawn Wilson "said that he thought the speech was a positive event" (p. 5).

Now when one considers what the Nation of Islam stands for, according to the speeches of its own national spokesmen, it makes DeAngelo X's claim that Ms. Pope was "ridiculing his religion" by referring to a publication by this group "as an example of 'radical' Afrocentrism" a bit hard to swallow.

It is also interesting to note that it was also reported that Mr. X had "not been back to class." It seems that he had "been arrested and charged with theft for trying to cash stolen cashier's checks—one for more than $500,000—taken from a bank in Iowa" (*Chronicle*, 1 December 1993, p. A-20).

As one sifts through Professor Pope's problems, Mr. X's behavior, the statements of people like Leonard Jefferies, Louis Farrakhan, and Khalid Abdul Muhammad, as well as the fact that "[Jesse] Jackson, [Congressman Kweisi] Mfume and the NAACP all ignore[d] Farrakhan's latest slurs against Jews," I think Jonathan Alter's point that all this "undermines their moral authority in fighting racism" is well taken (*Newsweek*, 14 February 1994, p. 48).

There remains one more interesting irony to be discussed involving Farrakhan's Nation of Islam. Louis Farrakhan apparently participates regularly "in 'Salute to Malcolm X' ceremonies," which may sound reasonable to anyone who does not know that "it was members of the Nation of Islam who killed Malcolm X" (*Newsweek*, 14 February 1994, p. 48). But, this story gets even stranger. Reportedly, at two recent "rallies" commemorating Malcolm X, "Farrakhan brought Muhammad Abdul Aziz to the stage. Aziz spent 20 years in jail for his part in killing Malcolm X. . . . Malcolm X's family is appalled at Farrakhan's popularity" (*Newsweek*, 14 February 1994, p. 48). Confused? Well just remember that this is PC, and in PC antilogic is the rule. If it makes sense, it's probably not PC.

That same *Newsweek* article notes that "this fact [that it was members of the Nation of Islam who killed Malcolm X] is still almost unknown among younger African-Americans." Jonathan Alter, the author of the *Newsweek* piece also points out that "Spike Lee's gloss didn't help" to educate anyone about this circumstance. This, then, is yet another example of the distortion of history so typical of the politically correct phenomenon, and it apparently makes absolutely no difference how recent the historical event is.

Speaking of the difference between PC history and fact, let us consider "rap music," "which began as a fierce and proudly insular music of the American black underclass. . . . It is both a recreational vehicle and a form of social commentary: you can dance to it . . . and think it over too" (*Time*, 19 October 1992, p. 70). The *Time* article also maintained that rap "sounds like reggae on megavitamins, bulked-up and bass-pummeled, and it has its origins both in the Caribbean and in an aggressive black awareness" (p. 71).

Newsweek magazine did a piece on rappers more recently. Take Snoop Doggy Dogg, for instance.

> To Eugenia Harris, the rapper Snoop Doggy Dogg is something of a role model. Eugenia is 13. . . . "He [Snoop Doggy Dogg] grew up like us and he says we're all in the same gang," she said. "To me, he's saying you gotta take what's yours." . . . In the cities and suburbs kids love Snoop Doggy Dogg because they think he's "real." (*Newsweek*, 29 November 1993, p. 62)

Taneika Archer, a seventeen-year-old African-American girl, said, "He tells it like it's supposed to be told" (p. 63). Snoop is referred to as "a local hero," and as "the fastest-rising star in the music world" (p. 62).

The *Newsweek* article also featured Tupac Shakur, who is described as

> a shockingly handsome 22-year-old, a successful rapper and a gifted, formally trained actor. For his performance in John Singleton's film *Poetic Justice*,

he earned an NAACP Image Award nomination;
his current hit single, "Keep Ya Head Up," is cited
as an inspiration for young black women (p. 62).

According to Newsweek, "in 1993, the face of rap
music belonged to Dr. Dre, 28, a producer and rapper
from Compton, Calif., whose hard-core gangsta album,
The Chronic, outsold those by mainstream acts like Barbra
Streisand, Aerosmith, or Sting, and dwarfed all other
rappers" (p. 63). Dr. Dre is referred to in the article as
Snoop Doggy Dogg's "mentor."

Time also claimed that rap "is a certifiable, global
rhythm revolution. . . . The music is punchy, insinuating
and prime for export" (19 October 1992, p. 71). *Newsweek*
also did a piece on rappers entitled "The Postures and
the Reality." What you have just read is the "posture."
Now for some reality.

In November of 1993, Snoop Doggy Dogg "was in-
dicted in Los Angeles Superior Court for the murder of
Phillip Woldemariam. . . . [He] is currently free on $1
million bail" (*Newsweek*, 29 November 1993, p. 62). Mr.
Dogg has done prison time before, "for possession of
cocaine for sale."

Dr. Dre, "a former member of the notorious rap crew
N.W.A. (Niggaz With Attitude). . . , recently settled a well-
publicized suit for allegedly beating up rap-TV host Dee
Barnes in a Los Angeles nightclub" (*Newsweek*, p. 63).

In perhaps the most ironic case of all, Tupac Shakur,
who "is cited as an inspiration for young black women,"
was "arrested [with] two associates on charges that they
forcibly sodomized and sexually abused a woman in a
midtown [New York] hotel" (*Newsweek*, p. 62).

The disturbing reality, however, does not stop with
the alleged criminal behavior of these "role models" and
"local heroes." As George Will pointed out in a 1993
issue of *Newsweek*,

> When journalism flinches from presenting the raw
> reality, and instead says only that 2 Live Crew's
> lyrics are "explicit" and "controversial" and "pro-
> vocative," there is an undertone of approval. Ant-

onyms of those adjectives are "vague" and "bland"
and "unchallenging." . . . Only a deeply confused
society . . . [would] legislate against smoking in res-
taurants [while maintaining] singing "Me So Horny"
is a constitutional right.

What about calling Rodney King a "black motorist" as
though all this man had ever done was simply drive his
car around? Can that, too, be considered an example of
"journalism flinching from presenting the raw reality"?
Or what about when

> political figures [and some in the media] . . . re-
> ferred to the L.A. riot as a rebellion, implying that
> the rioters were somehow political heroes strug-
> gling against oppressive despotism . . . [when] . . .
> they grabbed electronic gear and liquor . . . [rather
> than] . . . food and baby goods, [and when] . . .
> one looter was quoted in the Los Angeles Times:
> "I just wanted free stuff like everyone else."

In fact, "only one suspect in the hundreds of cases
reviewed by the *Times* even invoked the name of Rodney
King," and he was *white!* As Mortimer B. Zuckerman,
editor-in-chief of *U.S. News & World Report*, said, "To
excuse such criminal behavior leads every law-abiding
citizen to think that authority has sacrificed both its moral
and practical resistance to crime" (31 May 1993, p. 82).

Before the PC crowd dismisses Mr. Will's and Mr.
Zuckerman's comments as "white, Eurocentric racism,"
they should consider the statements of Nathan McCall, a
black reporter for the *Washington Post*. Mr. McCall said,
"We need to acknowledge that there are obviously some
correlations between the constant, negative, violent messages that are being put out in rap and the violence that
exists out there in the real world" (*Newsweek*, 29 November 1993, p. 64). In that same *Newsweek* article, Jesse
Jackson is quoted as saying, "We're going to take away
the market value of these attacks on our person. Anyone
white or black who makes money calling our women
bitches and our people niggers will have to face the wrath

of our indignation" (p. 64). Right on, Reverend! Let us pray it is not too late.

An interesting aside to the whole issue of rap music is this. According to a story in the 3 November 1993 issue of the *Chronicle of Higher Education*, researchers in neurobiology at the University of California at Irvine wanted to study the effects of different kinds of music on intelligence and learning. The researchers reported their findings in a letter to the journal *Nature*. The research team found that "college students who had listened to Mozart's 'Sonata for Two Pianos in D major' before taking an IQ test scored eight to nine points higher." Gordon Shaw, a professor of physics at Irvine and a member of the research team said, "There are certain neurological firing patterns that occur when people are doing high levels of abstract reasoning. The music presumably excites these same, very structured, patterns." Conversely, "extremely repetitive music would have a 'very negative' effect on learning." Frances Rauscher, a research fellow at the University of California at Irvine's Center for Neurobiology of Learning and Memory, said, "It [extremely repetitive music] would sort of burn out those neural patterns [that occur when people are doing high levels of abstract reasoning] instead of enhancing them" (p. A-37). Let's see, "extremely repetitive music . . . burn[s] out those neurological firing patterns that occur when people are doing high levels of abstract reasoning." Hmmm. "Extremely repetitive music . . . burns out neurological firing patterns." Imagine that. Not only is much of rap just plain filthy, it may not be art at all. Or, if it is, it's a very, very, very low form. The question posed in the *Chronicle* article was, "Does Mozart make students smarter and repetitive music make them dumber?" The article then states, "Fans of rap [and all other forms of 'extremely repetitive' music] probably don't want to hear the answer" (p. A-37).

I appeared on a television show in New Orleans to discuss my first book on this subject which turned out to be a debate. The opponent that the show had selected to face me was Ron Mason, an African-American and the vice-president of academic affairs at Tulane University. During this program, I reiterated what I had stated in my book that it is time that black America start analyzing to what extent it is victimizing itself. After all, the illegitimacy rate for blacks is hovering around 70 percent. Are white men responsible for that?

I referred to a black man by the name of Ben Carson, whom I had mentioned in my first book. I had heard Mr. Carson speak in my town, and I had been impressed by him. Mr. Carson said that black America was suffering from what he called "The Crabs in the Barrel Syndrome." He said that if you put a bunch of crabs in a barrel and one of them starts to climb out, the others reach up and pull him back down. This was his analogy for blacks who tend to ostracize other blacks who become successful and dare to question the hegemony of the mainstream civil rights establishment.

Mr. Mason responded by saying that he "would not be held responsible for some dumb thing some dumb black guy said." I then informed Mr. Mason that Ben Carson, to whom he had just referred as "some dumb black guy," was the chief of pediatric neurosurgery at Johns Hopkins University. We should all be so "dumb."

Even Jesse Jackson has said, "We have lost more lives to the BBB than to the KKK. You all know who the BBB is. He is the Bad Black Brother" (*U.S. News & World Report*, 8 November 1993, p. 100). Now, when I said things like this in my first book and in my two campaigns for Congress, I was called a racist, but I have swallowed my frustration and decided that Plato was right when he said that it doesn't matter finally who gets credit for pointing out the truth, so long as it gets pointed out and, even more importantly, so long as something gets done. Besides, if I thought my frustration was bad, I can only imagine how the former U.S. vice-president felt when in a *Newsweek* article entitled "Endangered Family," Wallace Smith, black pastor of Shiloh Baptist Church in Washington said, "Dan Quayle was right" (30 August 1993, p. 20).

I suppose it is appropriate that blacks get credit for

solving their own problems, and who better than Jesse Jackson. The good reverend is the one who said to young blacks, "You're not a man if you can make a baby; you're only a man if you can raise a baby." According to *Newsweek*,

> Jackson increasingly aims his speeches at the most basic moral issues among his people: black-on-black violence, the disappearance of families and religious values in city slums, the silent, corrosive assent of students to guns and drugs in urban schools. To stop the murder, he says, blacks must undergo a "social-values revolution." (10 January 1994, p. 24)

Then, in a shockingly honest admission in that same *Newsweek* article, Jackson "confessed he is 'relieved' when he finds himself being followed on a street by a white person rather than a black."

Further evidence of encouraging progress in this "attitude adjustment" that seems to be gaining momentum is contained in a 15 November 1993 *Newsweek* article.

> In private, blacks are willing to concede that they sometimes take the victim thing too far.... That means focusing on whether Mike Tyson is a target of racism, instead of whether he committed rape. It means the National Association of Black Social Workers would rather see black orphans go unadopted than allow them into white families, which might dilute their "ethnicity." And it means that black professionals sometimes attribute to racism setbacks that may be the result of lack of merit or honest competition or just bad luck. (p. 54)

Clarence Thomas made some very striking points in a speech in May of 1993 at Mercer University in Georgia. He said:

> When I left Georgia over 25 years ago, the familiar sources of unkind treatment and incivility were the bigots. Today, ironically, a new brand of stereotypes and ad hominem assaults are surfacing across

the nation's college campuses, in the national media, in Hollywood, and among the involuntarily ordained "cultural elite." And who are the targets? Those who dare to question current social and cultural gimmicks. Those who insist that we embrace the values that have worked and reject those that have failed us. Those who dare to disagree with the latest ideological fad.

. . . During the 1980s, I watched with shock and dismay how friends were treated for merely disagreeing with what my friend Tom Sowell referred to as the "new orthodoxy." As a black person, straying from the tenets of this orthodoxy meant that you were a traitor to your race. You were not a real black, and you were forced to pay for your ideological trespass—often through systematic character assassination, the modern-day version of the old public floggings. Instead of seeing signs on public doors saying "no coloreds" allowed, the signs I saw were "no conventional ideas allowed."

. . . Does a black man instantaneously become "insensitive," a "dupe" or an "Uncle Tom," because he happens to disagree with the policy of affirmative action? . . . Does it make sense to criticize someone who says all blacks look alike, then praise those who insist that all blacks think alike?

. . . It is imperative that we recognize that where blacks were once intimidated from crossing racial boundaries, we now fear crossing *ideological* boundaries. And the intolerance and incivility that fuel both types of intimidation are reprehensible.

. . . Women have the right not to agree with the feminist agenda, and not to be personally attacked for it. Blacks have the right to criticize welfare policies, and not to be lashed by the cultural elite for doing so. . . . If we lose this battle, we risk finding ourselves once again judged not for our individual ideas or conduct, but only for our skin color or some other "immutable characteristic." (*The Wall Street Journal*, 12 May 1993, p. A-15)

Again, it is extremely important, in my view, that blacks are now saying these kinds of things, for their salvation is ultimately in their own hands. That's what America is all about. They wanted an equal share in the "dream," the chance to participate. Fine, that means you have the same chance as everyone else, and that means the chance to fail as well as to succeed.

Still, the most disturbing aspect of this whole "African-American" movement is how very divisive it is. As I stated in my introduction to this chapter, there can be no denying that the color lines that existed before the civil rights movement began are being redrawn, and a new age of segregation has definitely begun. One cannot help but sense the obvious resentment and bitterness that smolders just beneath the surface of the so-called Afrocentric movement. Sometimes that resentment and bitterness bubbles up, as it did in a piece published in our campus paper on 25 October 1991. Consider these excerpts.

> It is time African-American men stand up to this white racist society. . . .
>
> America is a country built on racism, discrimination and quotas. Four hundred years of free slave labor was the key factor which made this country the so-called great nation it is today. . . .
>
> Affirmative Action and quotas are insults to African-Americans viewing the opportunities and freedoms their ancestors have been denied, and are still being denied, since the time your racist forefathers created this vicious system to keep African-Americans oppressed.

Now I cited this editorial in my first book, but more recently, at a "free speech rally on racism" on my campus where students were allowed access to an open mike, a black student said, "People really need to wake up and see because justice needs to be heard. Justice needs to be done and if it's not done, black people are going to riot all over them because I know I am one of them and I will riot" (*Vermilion*, 8 October 1993, p. 2). Another student at that same rally made the following statement.

As far as solutions go, I think one of the better solutions, one of the solutions that people do not want to hear, which is—I think black people need to completely separate themselves from the white race in order to better ourselves.

As long as they are near us, around us, we have problems. The only time black people excelled was when they were in Africa developing science and math and their own religions.

Once we separate ourselves, then and only then, can we become a great people like we were once before.

My position is that you cannot solve a problem if you don't even know what the problem is. Telling black kids that all their failures are the result of racism and the fault of white people is a pernicious deception that has already led to violence and can only lead to more. It is precisely this kind of Sophistic antilogic, which has become so pronounced on campuses all over the country, that lead Professor Henry Louis Gates, Jr., director of African-American studies at Harvard and one of the most prominent black scholars in the world, to remind those who would listen that "the invidious scapegoating of other ethnic groups only resurrects the worst 19th-century racist pseudoscience—which too many of the pharaohs of 'Afrocentrism' have accepted without realizing" (*Newsweek*, 23 September 1991, p. 47).

In an interview he did with me for my first book on this subject, Dr. Gary Marotta warned, "We are reinventing racial apartheid, and it's a mistake." Arthur Schlesinger also felt compelled to warn, "Afrocentrism in the schools is a symptom of a growing fragmentation that is threatening to divide our society" (*Chronicle of Higher Education*, 6 February 1991, p. A-6). With all due respect to Mr. Schlesinger, it is my profound fear that the "division" of which he speaks is not just a threat; it is here.

Shelby Steele, black author of *The Content of Our Character*, wrote a piece that appeared in the August 1992 issue of *Imprimis* entitled "The New Segregation." Mr. Steele made the following observations.

> Colleges and universities are not only segregating their campuses, they are segregating learning. If only for the sake of historical accuracy, we should teach all students—black, white, female, male—about many broad and diverse cultures. But those with grievance identities use the multicultural approach as an all-out assault on the liberal arts curriculum, on the American heritage, and on Western culture. They have made our differences, rather than our common bonds, sacred. Often they do so in the name of building the "self-esteem" of minorities. But they are not going to build anyone's self-esteem by condemning our culture as the product of "dead white males."

As I mentioned in chapter 1, I have been doing interviews all across the country concerning my research and writing on the politically correct phenomenon, and I have articulated the very simple solution every chance I get. The solution is just this: we must drop the hyphens and think of ourselves as human beings first, Americans second, and whatever else after that. Recently, a black man called in to a radio program I was doing and said, "It's easy for white people to say we're all Americans. And they still teach their kids that they're something else too, like Germans or whatever. And you do, too."

"Sir," I said, "you are simply as wrong as you can be."

I then told him that last year my youngest son had as his final-essay topic in his seventh-grade language class the following question: Why should America try to be more like France? I was most unhappy with the teacher who had made this very politically correct assignment, and I informed my son of that fact. We discussed the situation and decided that since it was the end of the school year, rather than go through the bureaucratic hassle of challenging the teacher, he would just do the paper and say what he knew the teacher wanted to hear. It is appalling how many of our kids find themselves in such predicaments at all levels of education today. Neverthe-less, I made sure my son knew that, even though our heritage is French, we are Americans and that France should be trying to be more like us.

I also informed the caller that a colleague of mine, also from this area and of French extraction, spent a summer in France. When she returned, she said, "Who told those smelly, little people that they were the standard bearers of civilization?"

I then told the caller that a black student who was taking a class with me last summer had been asked to play host to some visitors from Africa (I am not sure what country they were from). After spending a week with these bona fide Africans, he said one day in class that he had nothing in common with those people. "I'm not an African," he said. "I'm an American."

Right on, brother!

Chapter Five

◇

Genderism:
Beyond Equality

"To know is to f——!" This is the rallying cry of the gender feminists or genderists, according to *New York Magazine* (21 January 1991, p. 38). As I pointed out in my first book on this subject, "gender feminism" or "genderism" is another of the "isms" spawned by the politically correct movement. Those who can be identified as gender feminists are fond of quoting Simone de Beauvoir, who said, "No woman should be authorized to stay at home and raise children . . . precisely because if there is such a choice, too many women will make that one." This, of course, is further evidence of the hypocrisy so deeply rooted in PC thinking.

As I have carefully and consistently maintained, it is possible to be a feminist without being a politically correct genderist. In other words, it is impossible for a rational, thinking person to deny that this culture has been guilty of discrimination against women. However, when one moves from admitting that and supporting reasonable measures to ensure equality of opportunity for women to attacking "analytical thinking as part of male domination" and comparing "scientific investigation to the rape of nature" (which, believe it or not, has been done), then one has crossed the line from the sublime to the ridiculous, from standing for reasonable and even noble ideals and goals to man-hating extremism. Need examples to illustrate how far this has gone? Better buckle up.

As I just mentioned and as I pointed out in my first book on this subject, gender feminists have attacked "analytical thinking as part of male domination" and have compared "scientific investigation to the rape of nature." A set of "feminist scholarship guidelines" was issued by a project mandated by the state of New Jersey which declared, "Mind was male. Nature was female, and knowledge was created as an act of aggression—a passive nature had to be interrogated, unclothed, penetrated, and compelled by man to reveal her secrets" (*New York Magazine*, 21 January 1991, p. 38). But, there's more.

That same issue of *New York Magazine* also revealed that Swarthmore College issued a "training manual" for its students. According to this "manual," "acquaintance rape . . . spans a spectrum of incidents and behaviors ranging from crimes legally defined as rape to verbal harassment and inappropriate innuendo" (p. 39).

More recently, George Will reported on a similar set of published "rules regulating 'interactions' of a sexual sort" at Antioch College in Yellow Springs, Ohio. The published rule book is called *Sexual Offense Prevention and Survivors' Advocacy Program*. Beginning by declaring "the frequency of 'sexual violence' on campus 'alarming,' Antioch displays nice evenhandedness regarding eligibility for the coveted status of victim" (*Newsweek*, 4 October 1993, p. 92). Tongue-in-cheek notwithstanding, Mr. Will has hit on a very significant point. According to the way in which words and categories are being defined in the current debates, virtually anyone can claim victim status, and that status has become access to power and celebrity. Witness Anita Hill. This status also excuses criminal behavior. Witness Lorena Bobbitt, the Menendez boys, and those accused of beating Reginald Denny. But, back to the specific victimhood at issue, I think it is best simply to quote from Antioch's regulations and let you decide for yourself if we have "gone off the deep end." Here are some excerpts from *Sexual Offense Prevention and Survivors' Advocacy Program.*

> All sexual contact and conduct between any two people must be consensual; consent must be obtained verbally before there is any sexual contact or conduct; if the level of sexual intimacy increases during an interaction (i.e., if two people move from kissing while fully clothed—which is one level—to undressing for direct physical contact, which is another level), the people involved need to express their clear verbal consent before moving to that new level; if one person wants to initiate moving to a higher level of sexual intimacy in an interaction, that person is responsible for getting the verbal consent of the other person(s) involved before moving to that level; if you have had a particular level of sexual intimacy before with someone, you must still ask each and every time. . . . Asking "Do you want to have sex with me?" is not enough. The request for consent must be specific to each act.

> Do not take silence as consent; it isn't. Consent must be clear and verbal (i.e., saying yes, I want you to kiss me now).

> . . . Sexual contact includes the touching of thighs, genitals, buttocks, the pubic region, or the breast/chest area.

> . . . Insistent and/or persistent sexual harassment includes, but is not limited, to unwelcome and irrelevant comments, references, gestures or other forms of personal attention which are inappropriate and which may be perceived as persistent sexual overtones or denigration.

George Will asks, can you "imagine being charged with making a 'gesture' that was 'irrelevant' or 'perceived' as denigrating" (*Newsweek*, 4 October 1993, p. 92). Thank you, Anita Hill. Will goes on to make the point that "our nation opted for the moral deregulation of sex a decade before deregulating the airlines. About 20 years ago colleges, like a lot of parents, stopped acting *in loco parentis* regarding sexual matters." I mean, wasn't it easier when dorms were sexually segregated and males were not allowed above the first floor of the girls' residence hall and we had chaperones and stuff. However, Will continues,

> Official indifference about what students do with their bodies includes all organs except the lungs: about smoking, colleges are as stern as they once were about copulating. Health care may be paid for partly with a "sin tax" on cigarettes. A million abortions a year is a mere matter of "choice"—an achievement of the "pro-choice" movement—but choosing to smoke is a sin. Interesting.

In other words, "Yes you may unbutton that, but no you can't smoke after." Sorry, but there's still more.

Some academics suggest that "mutual consent" may not even be enough to prevent "sexual violence." Andrea Parrot, a professor at Cornell University, was quoted in *New York Magazine* as saying that "any sexual intercourse without mutual desire is a form of rape." The article points out that Professor Parrot did not say "mutual *consent*" but "mutual *desire*." The article concludes that this could be taken to mean that "a woman is being raped if she has sex when not in the mood, even if she fails to inform her partner of that fact" (21 January 1991, p. 38). It gets worse.

Alison Jaggar, a professor at the University of Cincinnati and the head of the American Philosophical Association's Committee on the Status of Women in Philosophy, maintains that a simple candlelight dinner is "prostitution." While she admits that "both man and woman might be outraged" by such a description, "the radical feminist argues that this outrage is simply due to the participants' failure to perceive the social context in which the dinner occurs" (*New York Magazine*, 21 January 1991, p. 38). Sorry, not done yet.

According to the *Chronicle of Higher Education*, Chris Robinson, a graduate student in clinical psychology at the University of Nebraska, was accused of sexual harassment. It seems that Mr. Robinson "had a photograph [5 x 7 inches] on his desk of his wife—softly lighted, wearing a chain-mail bikini. . . . Two female graduate students who shared an office with Mr. Robinson told him the picture created a hostile work environment for them and for the undergraduates who visited the office. It, therefore, constituted sexual harassment, they said." The chairman of the psychology department, John J. Berman, "agreed [with the two female graduate students] and told Mr. Robinson to remove the photo" (*Chronicle*, 16 June 1991, p. A-33). Again, sorry, but we're still not done.

A letter to the editor in the *Clarion-Ledger*, 4 October 1992, quoted the following "news item." "The American Association of University Women demands that Mattel Toys recall 'Teen Talk' Barbie because one of the phrases the doll utters is 'Math class is tough.' The AAUW says this 'is a sexist remark' and 'could discourage girls from success in math.' " The piece goes on to point out that not only is the logic that would lead to such conclusions amazing, no less mind boggling is that "the media continue to report this with the solemnity suitable to a bulletin from a war zone." Still not finished. You'd better sit down for this one.

Jan Schaberg, a professor of religious studies at the Catholic University of Detroit Mercy, has written a book "on the birth of Christ called *The Illegitimacy of Jesus* (Harper & Row, 1987). In it, she contends that Jesus's mother Mary was not a virgin who was impregnated by the Holy Spirit" (*Chronicle of Higher Education*, 6 October 1993, p. A-7). Professor Schaberg, a former nun (member of the Religious of the Sacred Heart), concludes that, "Mary was raped." In a *Time* magazine article entitled "Handmaid or Feminist," Ms. Schaberg is quoted as saying that "the unwed Mary was impregnated by a man other than fiancé Joseph and that she was a liberated woman who was 'not identified or destroyed by her relationship with men' " (30 December 1991, p. 66).

As I mentioned in my introduction, a Maryland art expert maintains that da Vinci's Mona Lisa "could have been a battered woman." Jacob Borkowski claims that "the physiognomy of the subject of da Vinci's portrait . . . suggests she was missing teeth. His analysis also revealed signs of scar tissue around her mouth. 'She isn't smiling,' says Borkowski. 'Her expression is typical of people who have lost their front teeth'" (*Newsweek*, 22 November 1993, p. 10). Where will it all end?

As with all other manifestations of the PC lunacy, gender feminism is no longer only on college campuses. *Newsweek* reports that "even at the high-school level, groups like FURY (Feminists United to Represent Youth) and YELL (Youth Education Life Line) are launching campaigns for better sex education, blowing the whistle on sexual harassment and fighting stereotypical female images." Furthermore, "the National Abortion Rights Action League operates a nationwide campus-organizing effort, and the National Organization for Women now boasts a smattering of high-school chapters" (27 September 1993, pp. 69–70).

NBC's "Dateline" 8 February 1994 program featured a segment on gender bias against girls in high schools. According to the "experts" on the program, instructors favor male students in coed situations, and girls don't raise their hands as much in mixed groups. Girls, the experts claimed, do better in single-sex classrooms, especially in math and science. Now the only way to demonstrate the validity of such a position is to establish study groups, one all-girl class and one coed class. Both groups should be responsible for the same material and should take the same tests. The test scores can then be compared, and the validity of the position verified or refuted. That's what they did.

According to "Dateline," the instructor took more time with the girls in the all-girl class, and there was more "hands-on" interaction. The girls in the all-girl class asked more questions, and the students worked in groups to solve problems rather than on their own. That all sounds fine, but the all-girl class did not cover as much material as the coed group, and *the final test scores were not given!* In other words, after going through all the intricacies of classroom interaction between instructor and student in two different situations, no basis was given for finally determining whether the original position was correct or not.

The "Dateline" program reveals two problems with the whole politically correct phenomenon and with genderism specifically. First, so many PC claims are based on nothing that even remotely resembles science, and, when evidence is forthcoming which refutes their positions, they simply ignore it and maintain their position; such is the nature of sophistic antilogic. Secondly, while it is being maintained that girls function better in all-female situations and enrollment at all-girl schools is, according to "Dateline," at its highest levels in fourteen years, females are suing for admission to all-male universities and institutions, especially military ones. Now let's see if we've got this straight. It's okay to have all-girl institutions, but if girls want to get into all-male schools, that's okay too. How convenient. As is the case with so much of the politically correct movement, the hypocrisy is glaring.

Genderism, this radical, aggressive form of feminism, is based upon the premise "that Western society is organized around a 'sex/gender system.' " According to Sandra Harding, a professor of philosophy at the University of Delaware, central to this sex/gender system "is male dominance made possible by men's control of women's productive and reproductive labor" (*New York Magazine*, 21 January 1991, p. 38). So, as I pointed out in my first book, abortion is a central issue for this PC group.

The politically correct position on abortion is, of course, the "prochoice" posture. It is interesting to note that political correctness and prochoice have the same initials. Nevertheless, it has always seemed to me that the prochoice gender feminists let men off too easily. The availability of cheap, legal abortions and the position that it is simply a woman's "choice" takes men completely out of the loop and allows them to act irresponsibly with impunity. Women, after all, still cannot impregnate themselves or each other, at least not yet. So, it stands to reason that a pregnancy presupposes a "choice" by a man too. Why let them off so easily? Perhaps that is why Professor Christina Sommers has written that some of their positions "make gender feminists . . . oddly unsympathetic to the women whom they claim to represent" (*New York Magazine*, 21 January 1991, p. 38).

Discussion of this issue will also quickly reveal three other aspects of the politically correct phenomenon as it has developed in this country. First, the PC crowd's knee-jerk resorting to *ad hominem* attack to refer to anyone who dares dispute any item on their agenda. Second, their penchant for the use of misleading euphemism when referring to their own positions and agenda. Third, the mainstream media's political correctness. Allow me to demonstrate.

By calling themselves "prochoice" or "abortion rights activists," this arm of the PC movement accomplishes two things. First, they avoid the label "proabortion," which has more negative connotations than "prochoice." Second, the euphemism "prochoice" renders opponents, *ipso facto*, "antichoice" or "antirights." The mainstream media, of course, cooperates in this little verbal sleight of hand by always referring to the proabortion forces by the names that group has chosen for itself (i.e., prochoice or abortion rights activists). But, never have I heard a single report in the mainstream media on this issue in which abortion opponents are referred to as "prolife," which is the designation they have chosen for themselves. I suggest that this discrepancy is not subtle.

Some in the proabortion camp have even come to actually rationalize their position in this way, i.e., as "prochoice" rather than as proabortion. I have heard so-called prochoice people say, "I personally believe abortion is wrong, and I wouldn't have an abortion, but I don't want to infringe on someone else's right to have an abortion." This kind of rationalization is typical of sophistic antilogic and modernist thinking, in which the roots of the politically correct phenomenon are so deeply embedded. The notion, of course, is that since there is no such thing as universal truth, and any position is only a matter of personal opinion which is based on a cultural bias. Therefore, while I can say that something is wrong for *me*, I cannot say that it is wrong for *you*. There are, of course, several serious philosophical problems with this position.

First of all, to take the position that abortion is wrong but, at the same time, be unwilling to take a stand against it means that the individual does not really have the courage of his or her convictions. Henry David Thoreau, Mohandas Karamchand Gandhi, and Martin Luther King, Jr., all agree on this point. To recognize something as wrong and to do nothing to oppose it is to participate in the injustice.

Second, consider the following statement. "That which is not just is not law. I am in earnest. I will not equivocate. I will not excuse. I will not retreat a single inch, and I will be heard. This is sin. Those who maintain it are criminals." Now, I am fond of reading passages and then asking my audiences to identify the writer and the context of the comments. When I ask people to do that with this quotation, most say that it sounds like some right-wing, evangelical, Bible-thumping preacher talking about abortion. I agree. It does, indeed, sound like that, but it's not.

The preceding statements appeared in 1831 in *The Liberator*, a Boston, antislavery newspaper. The statements were written by William Lloyd Garrison, a noted abolitionist. Comparing the abortion issue to the slavery issue yields some more very interesting results, for anyone who is logical and open-minded enough to do it.

The position, for instance, that "I think abortion is wrong, and I wouldn't have one, but I wouldn't want to infringe on someone's else's right to have one" is *exactly and precisely* the same position taken by the apologists for slavery in the nineteenth century. It is also interesting to note that the abolitionists, those who took the position

that slavery was morally wrong and wanted to put an end
to the institution once and for all, were accused of being
"right-wing fanatics" who were attempting "to infringe on
other people's rights by seeking to impose their values."
Sound familiar? Most people took the position that, "I
think slavery is wrong, and I wouldn't own a slave, but I
won't interfere with someone else's right to own a slave."

There are other compelling comparisons between the
twentieth century issue of abortion and the nineteenth
century issue of slavery. There were many attempts made
to resolve the slavery problem politically. Legislative attempts included such bills as the Three-fifths Compromise, the Missouri Compromise, the Compromise of 1850,
and the Kansas-Nebraska Act. There were also judicial
decisions on the issue of slavery, the most famous of
which involved Dred Scott.

Slavery was an issue, however, that simply would not
be compromised away. The abolitionists, those right-wing
extremists, were not to be satisfied or silenced. Their
position was simple and uncompromising. Slavery was a
moral issue, not a political one, so any attempt to resolve
it politically (i.e., by legislative compromise or judicial
precedent which stopped short of abolition) was begging
the ultimate question and, therefore, a waste of time.
Slavery was wrong, morally wrong, and needed to be
abolished, period. That, by the way, was also the position
taken by Abraham Lincoln in the famous debates with
Douglas. He said that slavery was "a moral, a social, and
a political wrong" and that "it was the duty of the federal
government to prohibit its extension into the territories"
and to "put [slavery] in the course of ultimate extinction."
No serious student of history can ignore the compelling
parallels between the abortion controversy of the twentieth century and the slavery issue of the nineteenth century.

Like slavery, abortion is an issue that simply refuses
to go away, in spite of repeated legislative and judicial
attempts to resolve it by compromise. Like the abolitionists of the nineteenth century, if one perceives abortion

to be morally wrong and accepts the positions articulated by Henry David Thoreau, Gandhi, and Martin Luther King, Jr., then there is no room for compromise, and the position that it is wrong but we cannot interfere with people's right to choose to do it becomes a moral "cop-out."

By the way, it is interesting to point out, just as an aside, that it was white males who died by the thousands to accomplish the noble goal of eliminating slavery, and that it was a white, male Republican president who issued the Emancipation Proclamation, *and* that it was a white, male Republican Congress that passed the Thirteenth Amendment to the Constitution abolishing slavery once and for all and forever. A reasonable person might be inclined to ponder the inconsistency of demanding that we politically incorrect white males accept the blame for the sins of those of our fathers who participated in the institution of slavery while we are given no credit whatso-ever for the heroism and sacrifice of those of our fathers who died to end it, and there were many, many more of the latter than the former. A reasonable person might be inclined to view this not only as an inconsistency, but as an injustice. Nevertheless, there is yet one more compel-ling similarity between abortion and slavery that needs to be discussed.

The simple fact is that no "right" is absolute. While we are guaranteed freedom of speech, we do not have the right to "shout fire in a crowded theatre." The premise is, again, very simple. Your rights are limited by my rights, and vice versa. In other words, your freedom to swing your arm stops at my nose. To defend your rights by denying mine is to dehumanize me. The only way that one could take the position that slavery was wrong but that it would not be proper to interfere with someone's "right to own a slave" would be to dehumanize the indi-vidual who was the slave. And, that is exactly what hap-pened. Those who saw nothing wrong with their owning slaves as well as those who could not bring themselves to oppose slavery on the grounds that it would be interfering with the slave owner's rights were *both* guilty of dehumanizing the victim, the Negro. To regard the Negro as a human being and to refuse to deny someone the "right" to own that human being would be morally reprehensible.

The Nazis, of course, applied the same kind of sophistic reasoning to excuse the Holocaust. In their minds, there was no more morality involved in exterminating Jews than there was in having Orkin exterminate bugs in a home because the Jew, after all, was not a human being. In other words, the only way anyone can rationalize perpetrating something like slavery or the Holocaust or not opposing such things with all the moral strength one can muster is to dehumanize the victim. That way we can talk about the perpetrators' rights without violating or even considering those of the victim. It would seem that proabortion forces are committing the same error.

The only way that any decent person can defend anyone's right to an abortion is to deny the humanity of the unborn because any decent human being understands that ending someone else's life is not and cannot be merely a matter of "choice." That, of course, leads to the ultimate question. What is a fetus? In my mind, there is no other issue in this whole debate, and so it was with slavery.

If a Negro is a human being, it is wrong to own him or her, and no one has the right to do so. If a fetus is a human being, it is wrong to take his or her life, and no one has the right to "choose" to do so. So, let us seek to examine the nature of a fetus, as I did in my first book on this subject, and I would suggest now as I did then that it would be appropriate that such an evaluation be logical, rational, and scientific rather than political.

The simple fact is that advances in medical technology have not been kind to the proabortion forces. Ultrasound imagings, for instance, show very clearly forms that appear hauntingly human doing "baby things" like sucking thumbs much earlier in gestation than was formerly believed.

Another issue that has arisen which would seem to pose problems for proabortion advocates involves a technique developed and practiced in Europe whereby eggs taken from unborn fetuses are then fertilized and implanted in the uteruses of women who want to have children but cannot. The procedure has already been done successfully in mice. The reason this would seem to be troubling to proabortion advocates, especially feminists, is that now these "unviable tissue masses," which is how they have always referred to the fetus, can be identified as females that are capable of reproducing. Rush Limbaugh asked where people born under such circumstances would go on Mother's Day. I have an even tougher question. Where would they go on Grandparent's Day?

Nevertheless, it has also been established that a fetus has brain waves that can be measured by EEG only forty days after conception. Furthermore, fetal heartbeat is measurable merely eighteen days after conception. But, it gets even worse for the proabortion advocates.

Genetic research is now all the rage, especially with recent media attention paid to so-called cloning in laboratory tests. DNA identification is now being used more and more in criminal investigations, and the courts are now admitting such identification as evidence. The reason is that DNA structure, which is contained in virtually every cell in the human body, is unique to every individual, and this type of identification is much more accurate than the traditional finger print. In other words, DNA contains a genetic finger print that distinguishes each individual from all others who are alive, have ever lived, or will ever live, and virtually every cell in your body has the same DNA code. Here's the problem.

Scientists can construct precisely what an entire individual will look like with a single cell from an embryo *three days after conception*. Even worse for the proabortion forces is that at the moment of conception, the cells that make up the embryo are different from the mother's, so that "unviable tissue mass" is *not* part of the mother's body but a genetically distinct individual. It must be stressed that these are *not* personal opinions or political positions, but scientific facts that no amount of marching, speechifying, legislating, and/or litigating will ever change.

I think that we should also be quick to point out that anyone who bombs an abortion clinic or shoots a doctor who performs abortions becomes guilty not only of a heinous act that simply cannot be condoned but also of the same hypocrisy that is so characteristic of the politically correct phenomenon. In other words, one cannot kill in the cause of "right to life."

That being said, it is interesting to observe how easily the politically correct shift into their denial mode when historical or scientific facts get in the way of their political and social agenda. When such facts mitigate against their positions, the PC crowd employs Stalinist tactics and either change them or ignore them. That is why the proabortion forces "freak out" when prolife forces carry pictures of unborn babies and aborted fetuses. Those are *facts* that they would rather not see. Still, it is difficult to understand how, given the scientific facts, proabortion advocates can continue to so completely dehumanize the fetus. Not only are the proabortion advocates able to rationalize their position as a political issue revolving solely around women's rights, they have even gone a step further in dehumanizing the fetus and now cheer Clinton's lifting a federal ban on the use of fetal tissue in research as a major step forward. It is absolutely mind-boggling to me that there are those who cannot or will not see that this kind of research is frighteningly reminiscent of the Nazi's "medical" experiments, and, in my view, those who cannot see the very real possibility of a black market developing to provide "tissue" for this kind of research are either hopelessly naive or very sophisticated. But, if one is prochoice, one must dismiss such a concern as silly and even hysterical.

Furthermore, I am still waiting for the prochoice gender feminists to promote, with the same virulence with which they advocate abortion rights, support groups for the women who have had abortions and who, in retrospect, deeply and passionately regret that decision and live in anguish, tortured by their "choice." I know as a matter of plain, simple, sober fact that such women are out there and that there are many of them. Because some of them are close, personal friends of mine, I can tell you with absolute authority that their pain is real and intense, and some of them feel confused. How can they speak of their pain without betraying the pro-choice movement? Here is yet another area where "gender feminists . . . [appear to be] oddly unsympathetic to the women whom they claim to represent" (Professor Christina Sommers, *New York Magazine*, 21 January 1991, p. 38).

Just as it appears that their positions on abortion send politically correct gender feminists crashing head-first into the wall of scientific fact, those positions also place them on a head-on collision course with politically correct multiculturalism. For instance, what would be the politically correct position for a gender feminist/multiculturalist to take on China's policy on forced abortions? Even more troubling would be the practices in India featured on a CBS "60 Minutes" program that aired in January of 1993.

Among these practices is the use of ultrasound to determine the gender of an unborn child so that the females can be aborted. Now, if one is a politically correct genderist, does one support the right of Indian mothers to "choose" to abort their female babies regardless of the reason for the choice, or does one criticize the misogynic culture that forces women into this position? Alas, if one chooses the latter position, one sins against politically correct multiculturalism for, as Eli Sagan pointed out in his lecture on my campus, "advocates [of] . . . cultural diversity [maintain that] no culture has the right to sit in judgment on another culture, or even particular aspects of another culture."

The reason this is done, of course, is because Indian society makes having a daughter an inconvenient and expensive proposition. In order to get young women married off, the family of the woman must provide a dowry for the groom. It was also presented on the "60 Minutes" broadcast that women whose families do not provide a rich enough dowry face the possibility of being killed. The most common method, according to "60 Minutes," is to set the woman on fire. Very graphic pictures were shown of victims, some still alive, quivering, with the flesh melted upon their bodies. But, again, one cannot criticize this culture for its practices without running afoul of politically correct multiculturalism.

Then, there is the ritual of "female circumcision," reportedly a "widespread procedure" in Africa, the Middle East, and Southeast Asia, and "even some women in the United States have endured some form of it" (*Newsweek*, 20 December 1993, p. 124). Estimates place the number of women who "have endured some form of it" between "85 to 114 million." The procedure is described in the *Newsweek* article.

> The details aren't in dispute: a girl, sometimes as young as an infant, has all or part of her external genitalia removed. That can mean excision of the clitoris and the labia minora. The surgeon—who typically isn't a doctor—scrapes the sides of the labia majora and stitches together the vulva with thread or thorns, all while the girls are awake and held down. The purpose, dating to ancient Egypt: to ensure virginity and eliminate sexual sensation, and thereby make women marriageable.

The name of this "procedure" is yet another example of politically correct euphemism. The practice should be called "female genital mutilation," as the *Newsweek* article points out. Nevertheless, here, again, a politically correct genderist/multiculturalist has a very serious philosophical problem because any position such a person would take would violate some PC "Thou shalt not." As *Newsweek* points out, the issue "pits . . . advocates of intervention against those who say Western do-gooders are guilty of cultural condescension." Fortunately, I have no problem engaging in "cultural condescension," and this little Eurocentric, homophobic, racist, sexist male says this practice is barbaric and inhuman, and cultures that engage in such practices are, to say the least, uncivilized, and they should *stop!* It's so much fun being politically incorrect and not caring if you offend barbarians who mutilate young girls. Unfortunately for the politically correct genderist/multiculturalist, "female circumcision" is not the only problem area where their "isms" run into each other.

It has always been and remains a complete mystery to me that while the PC feminists succeeded in moving sexual harassment to the front burner as a national issue, they have remained ominously silent over many of the lyrics found in rap music, lyrics that are not only so vulgar that they would offend even the most tolerant of individuals, but which also advocate unspeakable violence against women. Nothing in my experience goes further than the lyrics of some of these songs in reducing women to mere objects that exist solely for the purpose of satisfying male prurient desires. (For a more detailed discussion of the subject of rap music and musicians, see chapter 4—"Afrocentrism: Beyond Civil Rights.")

Another troubling question which a rational, thinking person could not help but pose is this. How far are the attitudes reflected in the lyrics of many rap songs from those that permit (and excuse) promiscuous, profligate males to impregnate many females but then support neither the mothers of their children nor the children that they sire? Are we, in the name of politically correct multiculturalism, to respect "cultures" that not only allow but encourage men to act irresponsibly with impunity and to victimize women and children in the process? It is difficult to forget the intensity with which the PC police attack those who question the "practices" and "customs" of other "cultures."

Nevertheless, perhaps it would be more logical to adopt the position that any culture that not only tolerates but encourages the abuse of its female members by allowing and even demanding that they be burned alive or mutilated physically or demeaned in filthy song lyrics or impregnated and then left to raise their offspring alone just might not be worthy of respect and should seriously reconsider its "cultural" mores. In other words, is it not more logical to adopt the position that cultures should be respected *only* insofar as they *deserve* respect? Furthermore, while it is clear that our culture is not perfect and that there is always room for improvement in everything, just what culture would the gender feminist/ multiculturalist have us look to for guidance in the area of women's rights? Do we look to the Middle East or the Far East or India or Africa?

The simple, politically incorrect fact is this: when it comes to attitudes toward women, no other culture on earth has moved further in advancing equal opportunity for women than the democracies found in America and Europe with their roots deeply embedded in Western civilization, and the fact that so many gender feminists refuse to recognize the incredible strides this culture has made toward equality of opportunity for women is yet another example of politically correct dishonesty and hypocrisy.

Not only do politically correct gender feminists refuse to admit that our culture is the most progressive in human history regarding women's issues, they maintain that, "most of Western culture . . . has been a testament to male power and transcendence, it is a moral evil dedicated to the enslavement of women and must be discarded." Predictably, the gender feminists see the traditional family as "dysfunctional" and "the cornerstone of women's oppression and would like to abolish the family altogether" (*New York Magazine*, 21 January 1991, p. 38). Let us proceed to analyze this view.

The PC crowd often points to such things as domestic violence, child abuse, and incest as proof of their position that the "traditional family is a dysfunctional unit." The television tabloid talk shows seem to be cooperating in the effort to leave us with the impression that such behavior is now the norm. What they don't seem to understand is that while such things do occur and are certainly examples of dysfunctional behavior, not *all* "traditional families" experience such things. As a matter of fact, I would go so far as to say that families that experience such things are *not* traditional families at all because families who live by traditional values do not engage in such behavior. The only thing that dysfunctional families that experience domestic violence, child abuse, and incest might have in common with a "traditional family unit" is that there are two parents in the home who are not of the same sex, but that is as far as the comparison goes. The PC crowd, however, in their usual dishonest way, would have us believe that a "traditional family" and a "dysfunctional family" are, in fact, synonymous, and that is simply not true.

It has even become very stylish to maintain that we no longer know what a "family" is. At such gatherings as the 1992 Democratic National Convention, for instance, it was suggested that there are so many kinds of "families," that we can no longer assume that the so-called traditional family is the norm. While I might concede a certain validity to that point, I must once again play the politically incorrect devil's advocate and examine the implications of this position.

The "traditional family" is a unit consisting of a male and a female who have had children either by normal biological processes or adoption. I would hope that we could at least agree on that, even if we were to admit that this "unit" is becoming an endangered species. The politically correct position is that this "unit" is nothing more than a political/sociological construct, created by men to oppress women. But, suppose, just suppose, that the "traditional family" is more than that. Suppose one begins from a biological premise rather than a political one. That is what I did in my analysis of the abortion issue, and that is what I propose to do now. Let us then examine the *biological* differences between men and women.

Women have organs that men do not have, and vice versa. Men and women have hormones in vastly different proportions. One might even accurately say that the dif-

ference in degree is so great that it becomes a difference
in kind. There is a commercial running now featuring the
actress who played Kevin Arnold's mother in the ABC
series "The Wonder Years." In that commercial, she lists
all the things that men will never experience, things like
menstrual cramps, premenstrual syndrome, breast can-
cer, etc. One might also list all the things women will
never experience, like prostate problems, all demonstrat-
ing, of course, the original premise that men and women
are different. While this may not be politically correct, it
is, nonetheless, a biological fact. Where this logically leads,
of course, is toward the conclusion that maybe, just maybe,
the "traditional gender roles" as well as the "traditional
family" that is based upon those roles just might be nothing more than a mere concession to biological differences
rather than a political/sociological construct.

I think Kay Ebeling said it best. Ms. Ebeling is a single
mother with a two-year-old daughter who lives in
Humboldt County, California. She is also a free-lance
writer who wrote a piece entitled "The Failure of Feminism," which was published in the 19 November 1990
issue of *Newsweek*. I provided excerpts from that piece in
my first book on this subject, and I regard Ms. Ebeling's
comments as so important that I quote her again.

> To me, feminism has backfired against women. In
> 1973 I left what could have been a perfectly good
> marriage, taking with me a child in diapers, a 10-
> year-old Plymouth and Volume 1, Number One of
> *Ms. Magazine*. I was convinced I could make it on
> my own. In the last 15 years my ex has married or
> lived with a succession of women. As he gets older,
> his women stay in their 20's. Meanwhile, I've stayed
> unattached. He drives a BMW. I ride buses.
>
> Today I see feminism as the Great Experiment
> That Failed, and women in my generation, its per-
> petrators, are the casualties. . . . Feminism freed
> men, not women.
>
> The main message of feminism was: woman, you
> don't need a man; remember, those of you around

> 40, the phrase: "A woman without a man is like a fish without a bicycle?" . . . It was a philosophy that made divorce and cohabitations casual and routine. Feminism made women disposable. So today a lot of females are around 40 and single with a couple of kids to raise on their own. . . . Feminism gave men all the financial and personal advantages over women.

> What's worse, we asked for it. Many women decided: you don't need a family structure to raise your children. We packed them off to day-care centers . . . put on our suits and ties, packed our briefcases . . . convinced that there was no difference between ourselves and the guys in the other offices. . . .

> How wrong we were. Because like it or not, women have babies. It's this biological thing that's just there, these organs we're born with. The truth is, a woman can't live the true feminist life unless she denies her child-bearing biology.

There it is again, that "biological thing," and the suggestion that the "traditional family unit" just might be more than a political/sociological construct. Politically correct thinkers, however, cannot and will not accept or even entertain such notions because they see virtually everything in political and social terms, and that is why their positions very often contradict scientific fact.

Another female writer who wrote a very compelling piece dealing with this same issue is Maggie Gallagher, a journalist and an unwed mother. Her piece was a comment upon the firestorm created by Vice-President Dan Quayle's remarks about the television character, Murphy Brown. Quayle, who is still the favorite whipping boy of the PC crowd, took the position that the major crisis facing the United States today is the disintegration of the traditional family, which may well be the root cause of most if not all our social problems today. The vice-president also suggested that the entertainment industry could be contributing to the undermining of the traditional family by featuring characters like Murphy Brown who "choose" to have children out of wedlock. In her piece entitled "A Real-life Murphy Brown," which first appeared in *The New York Times* in 1992 and was reprinted in *Cosmopolitan* magazine in January of 1993, Maggie Gallagher shares her "personal recipe for single motherhood." Here are some excerpts.

> It is too late for Murphy Brown, but after all, she's only a fictional character who doesn't matter so much. But it may not be too late for the many young professional women I interview who are actively contemplating raising children outside of marriage.
>
> If you're thinking of unwed motherhood, it helps to:
>
> 1. Have relatively affluent parents who got and stayed married themselves. That way you can rely on their marriage, rather than your own, to give your child the emotional and financial emergency support he or she needs. . . .
>
> 5. Expect to give up all the advantages of single life (freedom, romance, travel) and receive none of the advantages of marriage (emotional, logistical, and financial support).
>
> 6. Prepare for the nights when your child cries himself to sleep in your arms, wondering why his father doesn't love him.
>
> . . . When *Glamour* asked its readers to describe 'the highs and lows' of being single moms by choice, fully half expressed serious regrets. It is an even worse bargain for the children.
>
> Dan Quayle was right on target [*WHAT!?!*] when he said that marriage is the best social program ever invented for the protection of children.
>
> The evidence is now overwhelming. . . .
>
> As impressive as the evidence is, it doesn't capture the true cost of the collapse of marriage. Even the

many children in single-parent households who grow up with all the material accoutrements of a middle-class family are being deprived of one precious and irreplaceable thing: a father.

. . . Children not only need a father, they *long* for one, irrationally, with all the undiluted strength of a child's hopeful heart. To raise one's own child without a father may, at times, be a painful and tragic necessity, but it should never be just another life-style option.

Now, if Ms. Gallagher is anywhere near being right, it seems that a "traditional family unit" is not only "convenient" biologically for parents, it fulfills a need for the children as well, a deep, "irrational" need for a father as well as a mother. I would assume that the father would have to be a man and the mother would have to be a woman because a "family" with "same-sex parents," which is a PC agenda item, would still leave the children with a "gap," so to speak. Talking in these terms, however, again brings us to the position that the "traditional family unit" fulfills needs for all involved that go way beyond political and sociological concerns.

Both Ms. Ebeling and Ms. Gallagher speak from a position of authority because they have lived the "life-style" of which they speak, a "life-style" advocated and promoted by the feminist movement. What this also means is that insofar as they are being judgmental, they are judging themselves, which not only adds to their authority, it is a testament to their honesty. I, too, can speak to this issue with some authority because I, too, was a single parent.

When my first wife left me in 1983, I made it clear to her that while I might consent to divorcing her, I would not divorce my three children. I insisted and got a custody arrangement that resulted in my kids spending the vast majority of their time with me, not because my ex-wife did not want to be with the children but because of our respective employment situations. She worked in retail, which meant long hours, weekend shifts, and especially

long days during holidays. I, on the other hand, as a
university professor, was available to pick up the kids
after school and spend all holidays with them while their
mother worked. The kids spent so much time with me
that, when it became necessary for the court to make a
decision, I was awarded sole custody of my children, and
their mother subsequently moved away to another state.
The point is that I, too, functioned for a long time as a
single parent, and so I speak with compassion for those
who find themselves in this situation. But, as a former
single parent who is a male, I can tell you that both Ms.
Ebeling and Ms. Gallagher are right. Two parents are
better than one, period. Furthermore, men and women
provide fundamentally different kinds of support and fulfill
fundamentally different needs for kids. In other words,
when the PC folks attack the "traditional family unit" as
nothing more than a political/sociological phenomenon,
they simply could not be more wrong.

Perhaps, we can also talk about the "maternal instinct" as an instinct that has a genetic basis rather than
a political one. In other words, as Ms. Ebeling so eloquently suggests, the "maternal instinct" just might be
that, an "instinct," a "biological thing" and not "learned
behavior" at all. In other words, the fact that women have
babies, and many of them actually want to, may not be
the result of male oppression at all. To demonstrate this
point, I will now share some very personal information
with you, and I do so with my wife's permission.

I am happily remarried, and my present wife is not
only a lovely woman, she holds two college degrees (B.A.
and M.A. in English). She also studied theatre arts at the
Academy of the Performing Arts in New York. She has
been teaching for over ten years both in college and in
high school and has also served in the administrative
capacity of Dean of Students. She is, in other words, a
well-educated, professional woman with her own career.
She was also a feminist, and I emphasize the past tense.
Growing up and attending school in the sixties, seventies,
and eighties, she, too, absorbed the attitudes that Ms.

Ebeling speaks of in her article. Premarital sex is okay.
Living together without being married is okay. Abortion
is a "choice." Women should be independent. Women
should have their own careers. A woman doesn't need a
man to be a woman. A woman doesn't need to have a
baby to be a woman. A woman doesn't need to have a
husband to raise a family. And on and on and on. In fact,
when it came to having children, my wife's motto when
we got married was "This factory is closed."

We now have two baby girls, a two-and-a-half-year-old
and a one-month-old, to go with the three kids I brought
into the marriage, and, if we could afford it, she says she
would be very content to stay at home with the kids. Now
that my wife has had children, and the decision to do so
was *hers*, she is passionately prolife and can't believe she
allowed herself to be denied the joys of motherhood for
so long. She denied herself because she bought the politically correct feminist lines. *That* was the "learned" behavior, and the maternal instinct, which she denied for so
long, is the natural one. In other words, the PC folks have
everything *exactly* backward, including the behavior that
the genderists advocate is "learned" as opposed to natural. As Kay Ebeling said, "The truth is, a woman can't live
the true feminist life unless she denies her child-bearing
biology." It would appear that early feminists like Simone
de Beauvoir were also aware of this and, therefore, refused to recognize staying home and raising children as
a valid "choice" for women.

The problem as I see it is this. Again, as I said at the
beginning of this chapter, no thinking, rational person
can deny that there have been double standards for men
and women operating in this culture of ours. Guys who
"fooled around" were "studs," while girls who did were
"sluts." Obviously, that is a double standard, and it is
unfair. That's the easy part. The hard part, and the place
where we missed the boat, was in deciding how to rectify
the situation.

You see, there are *two* ways to remedy a double standard. In this case, we could apply the same standard to

men that we applied to women or apply the same standard to women that we applied to men. Unfortunately, we chose the latter. In other words, rather than demanding that men conduct themselves in the same way that we expected women to behave, i.e., in a decorous, restrained, civilized, and moral manner, we decided that it would be okay for women to behave like men, and we had a sexual revolution so now everyone can "fool around." As Ms. Ebeling suggests, in many ways, women victimized themselves by demanding "equal rights." Because women have babies and men don't, you know, that "biological thing," we are not and cannot be equal. Men can walk away from an unplanned and unwanted pregnancy much more easily than a woman can. Ironically, the women's movement, and particularly all the prochoice rhetoric, has made it even easier for men to simply walk away. I saw a PBS program that featured a discussion of women's issues by a panel of women, one of whom said, "Ten thousand years of civilization has demonstrated very clearly that the only way to hold men responsible for the children they sire is for women to restrict sexual activity within the confines of matrimony." But, the politically correct gender feminists are quickly removing that obstacle to male irresponsibility with their concerted and consistent attacks on the "traditional family," and they're not even satisfied with merely abolishing the family.

As they put it, the traditional family "imposes the prevailing masculine and feminine character structures on the next generation . . . [and] enforces heterosexuality [which] is responsible for the subjugation of women" (*New York Magazine*, 21 January 1991, p. 38). Now, before you unfurrow your brow and stop scratching your head, let me assure you that you did not misunderstand what you just read. The gender feminists assert that "heterosexuality is responsible for the subjugation of women." Look out biology; here we come! That's right, no longer are violations of biological fact merely implied in their rhetoric and positions; the gender feminists are willing to take on biology directly. What they ultimately envision is "a society where . . . one woman could inseminate another, men could lactate, and fertilized ova could be transferred into women's or even men's bodies" (*New York Magazine*, 21 January 1991, p. 38). This, of course, is a macabre, dystopian vision of a futuristic PC land. But, what is more realistic is that the logical extension of the attack on heterosexuality as being "responsible for the subjugation of women" is the attempt to legitimize homosexuality, which is also an integral part of the PC agenda.

According to the *Chronicle of Higher Education*,

> the work [in the field of gay and lesbian studies] is closely connected to other developments in the humanities, broadly grouped under the category of cultural studies. . . . The influence of . . . especially feminism and Marxism is relevant. Lesbian studies, in particular, are deeply related to the growth of women's studies in the last 15 years. (24 October 1990, p. A-4)

Eve Kosofsky Sedgwick, a professor of English at Duke University, has been called "part mascot, part earth mother to the gay-and-lesbian studies movement" (*Chronicle*, p. A-4). Professor Sedgwick is author of the books *Between Men: English Literature and Male Homosocial Desire* and *Epistemology of the Closet*. Her recent papers include "Jane Austen and the Masturbating Girl" and "How To Bring Your Kids Up Gay." Her work rests on the scholarship of the late French philosopher Michel Foucault, who, in his book *The History of Sexuality*, "argued that sexuality is 'socially constructed.'" Professor Sedgwick apparently accepts this notion and, in her latest book, according to a review in the *Chronicle of Higher Education*, "with its insistence on identifying dichotomies in the language used to describe sexual choice . . . clearly aims to deconstruct . . . she wants to question and 'destabilize' the categories by which sexuality is defined" (24 October 1990, p. A-6).

Not only is "deconstructing" gender roles and "destabiliz[ing] the categories by which sexuality is defined" clearly part of the PC genderist agenda, that effort is well under way.

Chapter Six

———————————— ◇ ————————————

The Gay Nineties: Beyond Tolerance

When I asked in my introduction if any of you were aware that Mark Twain was gay, I did not pose the question facetiously. According to *U.S. News & World Report* (27 September 1993, p. 14), Andy Hoffman of Brown University "is suggesting that Huck's [Huckleberry Finn's] creator was gay. At a recent conference, . . . Hoffman alleged that Mark Twain may have had romantic relationships with men in his bachelor days as a reporter in the West." Hoffman bases his "allegation" on the "fact" that some of Twain's associates in the 1860s reportedly had same-sex affairs. Hoffman also "notes" that "there are several coy references recorded about Twain's various male roommates. Still, Hoffman admits he has no definitive evidence."

No "definitive evidence" indeed! First of all, I am certain that all of us know people who have had same-sex affairs. In fact, several of my colleagues are openly gay. Does that mean that I am gay? If I correctly recall my logic courses from my days as an undergraduate, I think this would fall under the logical fallacy of "guilt by association." Furthermore, could some of the "coy references recorded about Twain's various male roommates" be *jokes*? Twain, after all, again if memory serves, was a humorist. But, as I have pointed out, the PC crowd has no sense of humor, unless, of course, the object of the joke is Ronald Reagan, Dan Quayle, or Christians. These folks obviously believe that any references to homosexual behavior *must* be profoundly serious, and only homophobes could joke about this topic.

When I mentioned Hoffman's "allegation" to one of my colleagues at the university, he informed me that this was not new, that, in fact, it has been suggested before that Twain may have had gay tendencies. My colleague also informed me that one of the "coy references" in *Huckleberry Finn* pointed to as "evidence" of Twain's gaiety was Jim (the escaped slave with whom Huck travels) calling to Huck, "Come on back to the raft, Huck honey." My impression was that no real scholar had ever taken this seriously, but again, there is nothing funny to the PC crowd about any item on their agenda. The more historical figures that can be pointed to as having been gay, no matter how silly the "evidence," the more it furthers the PC agenda regarding gay and lesbian rights. Just how much progress has the PC crowd made in this arena?

In my first book on this subject, I revealed the following developments. In the 24 October 1990 issue of the *Chronicle of Higher Education*, it was reported that a gay and lesbian faculty research group at the University of California at Santa Cruz organized a conference called "Queer Theory." Please understand that this was an "academic" conference devoted *entirely* to homosexual issues. As I mentioned in chapter 3, Teresa de Lauretis, a professor of the history of consciousness at Santa Cruz, said the goal was "to understand homosexuality not as a perversion or an inversion of normal sexual identity but as a sexual behavior and an identity on its own terms—as a cultural form in its own right" (p. A-6). Also in October of 1990, the fourth annual Lesbian, Bisexual, and Gay

Studies Conference was held at Harvard. The conference, which featured over two hundred papers and eight hundred participants, "was organized under the title 'Pleasure/Politics,' [and] spanned the spectrum, with a particular emphasis on how sexuality relates to race and nationality. Sessions addressed AIDS and the politics of fiction; lesbian pornography; homosexual marriages, past, present, and future; and matters of censorship" (p. A-6). There were also discussions of the relationships between gay and lesbian studies and women's studies. It was also reported in the *Chronicle* that study groups in the area of gay and lesbian studies for faculty members and graduate students now meet regularly at Yale. Furthermore, in 1989, the first Department of Gay and Lesbian Studies was created at the City College of San Francisco, and, in the spring of 1991, City University of New York opened its new Center for Lesbian and Gay Studies, "which will focus on research, curriculum development, and eventually offer degrees" (p. A-4). Understand that it is now possible to get a college degree in gay and lesbian studies. Finally, it was also reported in the *Chronicle of Higher Education* that Richard D. Mohr, professor of philosophy at the University of Illinois at Urbana-Champaign said, "It [gay and lesbian studies] is exploding; it's incredible the number of academic writing projects being born" (p. A-4). Professor Mohr is the general editor of a book series published by Columbia University Press, the first three volumes of which are on gay male theater, homoerotic photography, and lesbian literary theory.

As I said, those were developments recorded in my first book on this subject. Now for an update. Northern Arizona University offered a course in the spring of 1994 entitled "Transsexualism and Society." The course, "which [was to] look at gender roles and expectations based on a person's sex, . . . [was to be] taught by a graduate student who is a transsexual" (*Chronicle*, 5 January 1994, p. A-24). It was also reported in a radio newscast that students enrolled in the class would be required to cross-dress. The governor of Arizona, Fife Symington, called the course "an insult to the taxpayers" and added that the course "strikes me less as a serious intellectual endeavor than an obscene gesture directed from the ivory tower of the academy toward the hard-working men and women on whose labors it depends" (*Chronicle*, p. A-24).

Some of these courses are being offered by young professors out of necessity. That's right, necessity. The 15 February 1994 issue of the *Wall Street Journal* contained a story about Caroline McAlister, whose father is an English professor at California State University in Sacramento. He is a Milton scholar. Professor McAlister's daughter is now also Professor McAlister. Professor Caroline McAlister, while attending Yale, discovered and developed "a passion for her father's favorite writer, John Milton. . . . So she went to Emory University for a Ph.D. and a dissertation on Milton—just like dad" (p. A-6). But, what starts out looking like a touching "like father/like daughter" story takes a macabre and troubling twist.

Professor Caroline McAlister is now teaching at Salem College, a small women's school in Winston-Salem, North Carolina. She is reportedly in her fifth year and "is eager to win tenure and has taken her colleagues' hints. She has . . . nudged both her research and her courses toward more popular modern and women's literature; she recently attracted huge enrollment for a class on cross-dressing in film and literature" (*Wall Street Journal*, 15 February 1994, p. A-6).

Professor McAlister's story is important for two reasons. First of all, as I stated in my first book on this subject and have already reiterated in this one, things like tenure and promotion are being used to enforce politically correct scholarship and instruction. Secondly, even professors who are trained in more traditional areas and would prefer to concentrate both their research and teaching in such areas are being "nudged" in politically correct directions in order to protect their careers. While both these issues are very disturbing, we have not even begun to scratch the surface of the power of this particular aspect of the politically correct phenomenon.

In the spring of 1993, a gay-lesbian-bisexual student club applied for formal recognition at Southern Utah University. In the 24 March 1990 issue of the *Chronicle of Higher Education*, "a university spokesman said the administration would not block the club's bid for university recognition," even though students had circulated a petition that had been signed by thirty-five area business owners threatening to withdraw financial support from the university (p. A-4).

In April of 1993, stickers "bear[ing] the pink and black triangles that have become symbols for the gay-rights' movement," began "appearing on doors and desks at the University of Rhode Island's campus to let gays and bisexuals know they are safe and welcome. Diana Goodman, interim head of URI's affirmative action office . . . added that the campaign is a response to 'a sense of gay invisibility' on the campus" (*Chronicle*, 21 April 1993, p. A-4). Please note that it was the university's "affirmative action office" that is behind this "campaign." Can quotas for gays be far behind?

In the summer of 1993, "the Academic Council at Wright State University voted twenty-eight to two . . . to censure a professor accused of harassing a student." According to Martin Arbagi, an associate professor of history and the faculty member who was censured, "he received the rebuke for expressing the 'politically incorrect' view that homosexuals should not serve in the military." Professor Arbagi also accused graduate students of "misrepresenting research" that they had done "on the issue of gays in the military." Arbagi was quoted as saying, "People on the left think you can use fraudulent research for the right cause" (*Chronicle*, 16 June 1993, p. A-6).

The military, of course, has become a specific target of the gay rights movement, and the gays continue to gain territory on campuses across the country in this PC theatre of war. In November of 1993, "a federal appeals court . . . ordered the U.S. Naval Academy to grant a degree to a student it had expelled after he said he was gay" (*Chronicle*, 24 November 1993, p. A-24). Also in

November of 1993, the faculty of Princeton "voted to recommend that the institution end its participation in the Reserve Officer Training Corps [ROTC] unless the military ends all discrimination based on sexual preference by June 1994." This action was apparently taken to protest Clinton's "Don't ask, don't tell" policy. "Steven Greene, an assistant professor of psychology and one of the sponsors of the proposal, said it was important for colleges to protest the Clinton policy" (*Chronicle*, 11 November 1993, p. A-25). In December of 1993, "a state judge . . . ruled that public universities in New York must ban military recruiters as long as the armed forces discriminate against gay men and lesbians" (*Chronicle*, 1 December 1993, p. A-28).

In the fall of 1993, "the American Civil Liberties Union . . . sued [the University of South] Alabama in federal district court, challenging a state law that prohibits public colleges from providing money or space to gay-student groups." Ruth E. Harlow, "associate director of the Lesbian and Gay Rights Project at the ACLU," called the suit "an important case." Please note that the ACLU now has committed an entire branch to lesbian and gay rights. George Hite Wilson, a sophomore at Alabama and president of the Gay Lesbian Bisexual Alliance, was quoted as saying, "I think it's going to be one of the first landmark cases involving a gay and lesbian group and a state law" (*Chronicle*, 6 October 1993, p. A-30).

In December of 1993, "officials at Central Michigan University angered Christian student groups when they said that campus organizations could not bar gays from holding leadership roles." In response to protests, the university decided "to exempt Christian groups from the policy." The exemption "prompted a new set of complaints, this time from the Gay/Lesbian Association for Student Support" (*Chronicle*, 1 December 1993, p. A-37).

It was also reported that in the fall of 1993, "Stanford University's Memorial Church held its first ceremony for uniting a gay couple. . . . The event, which the church called a commitment ceremony but the couple called a wedding, prompted the church to adopt a policy allowing such ceremonies" (*Chronicle*, 1 December 1993, p. A-6). If there is any doubt as to the obvious next step, it was reported in the 5 January 1994 issue of the *Chronicle of Higher Education* that "five gay and lesbian employees have sued Rutgers University to force it to provide health benefits to same-sex couples." The group, four faculty members and one administrator, have also named the state of New Jersey in the suit, claiming both Rutgers and the state have "violated anti-discrimination laws" and are seeking benefits "retroactive to 1991" (p. A-19).

The *Chronicle* also reported that

> in 1992, the University of Iowa and Stanford University were among the first institutions to offer health and other benefits to gay and lesbian couples. In recent months, a parade of institutions has followed, including the Massachusetts Institute of Technology [M.I.T.], Columbia, Harvard, and Yale Universities, and the Universities of Chicago, Minnesota, and Vermont. (3 November 1993, p. A-17)

This, of course, serves as yet another example of not only inconsistency, but of hypocrisy as "most of the campuses have excluded [unmarried heterosexual couples] from the benefits" (p. A-17).

According to Majorie K. Cowmeadow, associate dean of general studies at the University of Minnesota and head of a campus committee on lesbian and gay concerns, the issue involves more than the benefits, much more. Cowmeadow said, "It's a recognition that the university is treating gay couples and their children the same as married couples" (*Chronicle*, 3 November 1993, p. A-19). It is in such statements that the real agenda of the politically correct gay rights crowd can be found, and this is where the serious public opposition begins. As Representative Michael A. Fox of Ohio said when gays and lesbians attempted to gain access to Ohio State University's family housing, "Gays and lesbians are free to live their lives and not be discriminated against. But, this is an attempt by militants who want to hijack public institutions. They want to use public institutions to sanction their relationships" (p. A-19). There can be no doubt that Representative Fox is right.

As I reported in my first book on this subject, accrediting agencies have adopted policies mandating a school's commitment to "ethnic diversity" be used in accrediting colleges and universities. When attempting to clarify its position on "diversity," members of the Western Association of Schools and Colleges found "the issue of gay rights prompted the most heated debate at the meeting" (*Chronicle*, 17 November 1993, p. A-25). Now, one might reasonably wonder what in the world gay rights has to do with "ethnic diversity," but one must remember that it is only important to be politically correct and not logically so. What is painfully clear is that, for whatever reason, gay and lesbian issues are, indeed, an integral part of the whole debate on "multiculturalism" and/or "diversity."

Finally, there is the story of the "Straight 'Coming Out' Dance," which appeared in the newspaper *Campus Report*. After gays on the campus at Columbia Basin College demanded and received funding for "their own club so that they could be 'proud' of who they were," the College Republicans decided to hold "a heterosexual dance so heterosexuals could be 'proud' of themselves too."

Ken Forsberg, College Republican president, said, "Although the idea [of the straight dance] was suggested jokingly to me, the more I thought about it, the more I liked it. . . . There's no reason we can't be proud of who we are too. If it is 'okay to be gay,' then it should be okay *not* to be gay." Sounds reasonable, but stay tuned.

When the College Republicans submitted the dance for approval, the administration at Columbia Basin College was reportedly "infuriated." Byron Gjurdy, dean of Student Services, and Steven Baer, director of Student Services, reportedly portraying the situation as "a question of sensitivity," told the College Republicans "that 'there was no way this dance could be held with this theme.' The College Republicans were told to either come up with another theme or not to have the dance" (*Campus Report*, January 1994, Vol. IX, No. 1, p. 1).

The activities director for the College Republicans, Aaron Deaver, said the administration's position amounted to "censorship of politically incorrect expression," and added, "If a gay club was to hold a homosexual coming-out dance, the administration would have shown up with a red carpet and *hors d'ovres* [*sic*]" (*Campus Report*, p. 8). Given the other events I have reported on concerning gay rights activities on campus, I would suggest that Mr. Deaver's position would be correct, logically, but not politically.

Nevertheless, the Columbia Basin College Republicans refused to give up on having their dance to "celebrate heterosexuality," and pressure from the administration continued. Forsberg maintains that he was called "nearly every night" by Gjurdy who kept "urging" that the dance be called off. Forsberg also maintained that when he refused to attend yet another meeting to discuss the dance, "Gjurdy threatened to have the campus security 'come and get him.'" It was also reported that Columbia Basin originally "refused to print the notice of the dance in the student bulletin," that "flyers for the dance that were posted on campus bulletin boards were constantly being torn down," that the college "threatened to revoke the College Republicans' school charter and expel them from the student government," that faculty members "who planned to chaperon the dance were warned to back off by members of the tenure review board," and that the "staff advisor for the club [the College Republicans] felt it necessary to resign after continual pressure from the tenure review board" (*Campus Report*, p. 8).

When two constitutional lawyers agreed to represent the College Republicans for free, the college's position that the dance could not be held with the heterosexual theme, which Forsberg said was "straight out of the Donna Shalala/Sheldon Hackney Cookbook," suddenly changed, and the dance was held. According to Forsberg, the evening was an incredible success. The dance was covered by local media, and so many showed up that people actually had to be turned away. Forsberg's parting shot was this.

> In a world where an increasing number of groups are receiving special rights, someone has to stand up for the rights of everyone else. The rights of a Christian person are just as important as the rights of an atheistic person. The rights of a white person are just as important as those of a minority person. The rights of a straight person are just as important as those of a gay person. (*Campus Report*, p. 8)

As with every other PC theatre of war, the battle over gay/lesbian rights is no longer confined to our school campuses. Firefights continue to flare up in courts all over the country. Lawyers in the command posts include attorneys for the American Civil Liberties Union, which, as already mentioned, has an entire branch devoted to the issues of gay rights, and another group called Lambda.

On the same day that Bill Clinton announced his policy on gays in the military, Lambda lawyers won a challenge to the Colorado "antigay initiative" (so dubbed by the mainstream media) when the state supreme court questioned the constitutionality of the referendum passed by voters in November of 1992. Lambda lawyers also "forced a Florida sheriff's department to rehire a gay deputy sheriff, required a New York hospital to reinstate an HIV-positive pharmacist and struck down a Kentucky sodomy law" (Joseph P. Shapiro, *U.S. News*, 2 August 1993, p. 31).

Joseph P. Shapiro, a reporter for *U.S. News*, wrote a story on this group called Lambda in which he stated, "Perhaps no other group of lawyers in the country is doing as much to stretch the American definition of family and sexuality as are the eight gay and lesbian staff attorneys at the group [Lambda] headquartered in New York." Mr. Shapiro's comment is very revealing as to the real agenda and ultimate goals of the gay/lesbian forces and those pushing gay rights initiatives in this country, as

is a Lambda case in Hawaii. Lambda lawyers assisted in
a case that led to the Hawaii Supreme Court decision last
May "that could open the door to same-sex marriages
there" (*U.S. News & World Report*, 2 August 1993, p. 31).

U.S. News & World Report magazine reported in March
of 1993 that "a battle over gay rights has removed the
smile from Irish eyes and endangered one of New York's
most beloved traditions," the St. Patrick's Day Parade.
According to *U.S. News*, "at the urging of [then] Mayor
David Dinkins, the parade permit was taken away from
the Ancient Order of Hibernians, the sponsor since 1838."
The reason was that the Hibernians "had refused to let
the Irish Lesbian and Gay Organization march with its
banner." Although a judge gave the parade permit back
to the Hibernians and the parade did go on, with the gay
Irish having a separate parade, the "biggest loser may be
the city of New York. Ray O'Hanlon, senior editor of the
Irish Echo, says parade spectators pump up to $40 million
into the city every year, but crowds are shrinking. Last
year only 350,000 attended, down from 2 million in peak
years" (*U.S. News & World Report*, 15 March 1993, p. 13).

Many communities across the country are finding
themselves under the gay gun when they, like the city of
New York, invoke the wrath of the PC homosexual forces
and are subjected to similar tactics. When Colorado voters passed its "antigay" amendment, "some scholarly
groups moved their meetings away from Colorado to
protest the measure" (*Chronicle*, 5 January 1994, p. A-24).
According to *Newsweek* magazine, after Cincinnati "voters
last fall rejected a law giving equal protection to gays,"
there were threats of retaliation by "irked activists." Those
threats became real when "the American Historical Association . . . decided to move its 1995 conference," which
"means a loss to the city of 4,000 visitors and $3 million."
It was also reported that "the American Library Association announced it would not hold its annual meeting in
the city next year." Note that the two organizations making the people of Cincinnati "pay" for what gay rights
activists would certainly call their "homo-phobia" are "aca-

demic" groups. The *Newsweek* article concluded with the warning that "Pro-gay forces plan to turn up the heat in the coming months."

From campuses to courtrooms to comics, the PC homosexuals continue to march (if they're military or militaristic) or to sashay (if they're not). In an article entitled "PC Comics," *U.S. News & World Report* informs us that "sexual politics is Topic A in the funny pages." The story reports that "a character in the popular strip 'For Better or For Worse' has revealed that he is gay," and that "Bloodfire, reputed to be the first HIV-positive superhero" will be "making his debut in June." The article also informs us that "the superhero population has plenty of gay do-gooders, including Northstar, who stepped out of the closet in January 1992." Mell Lazarus, author of "Miss Peach" and "Momma" and president of the National Cartoon Society, is quoted as saying that "gay issues [are] now entering animated consciousness" because "they're important social issues" (*U.S. News & World Report*, 3 May 1993, p. 16).

Of course, the entertainment industry has been dealing with these "important social issues" for quite some time. There are even bisexual characters in movies like *Basic Instinc*t and prime-time television shows like "L.A. Law." Recently, the sitcom "Roseanne" featured a scene in a lesbian bar with Roseanne kissing Muriel Hemingway. Even though I missed the episode, it was all over the national news, and it was reported that it was one of the "most watched" shows in television history. I heard a discussion of this between two disc jockeys (a male and a female) on the way to work one morning, and the female DJ said, "Well, hey, it happens in real life all the time." Now, this is about the most inane and irrelevant point that could possibly be made, and yet it is constantly used to excuse presenting all kinds of filth as "art". The logical, rational response to this is that people have bowel movements everyday too. Shall we put that on prime-time television as well? The male DJ made a very good point when he said, "We're becoming a nation of voyeurs." He's right.

But, if there's money in it, some producer will put it on the screen.

Speaking of making money in a politically correct way, ABC's Morton Dean reported on the 25 February 1994 program of "Good Morning America" that the fourth major bank in the United States is now offering credit cards for gays and lesbians. "One percent of what is charged on the cards is donated to groups which work for gay rights." Where will it all end?

Time magazine reported on 9 July 1990 that "Reform Judaism . . . became the first major U.S. religious body to adopt a national policy that sanctions homosexual behavior." The article also reported that "same-sex relationships were deemed acceptable for those with no 'conscious choice' but to be homosexual" (*Time*, p. 62).

This, of course, leads to the slippery and tricky discussion of the nature of homosexuality, indeed a hazardous sea to navigate for anyone who is more interested in being logically correct than politically correct. The question that many are now struggling with is whether homosexual tendencies are the result of conscious choices (preferences) or whether they are the result of genetic factors (orientation). The confusing thing about this question is that the homosexual community itself came up with *both* explanations, and the gays and lesbians now find themselves deeply divided over this issue.

It was the homosexuals themselves who first referred to their behavior as "sexual preference." Frank Aqueno, for instance, a gay free-lance writer, appeared on the "Donahue" program that focused on this topic and boldly proclaimed that his homosexuality was a "conscious, rational choice." The problem, of course, is that if homosexual behavior is a result of "preference," a "conscious, rational choice," then there are ethical and moral implications, assuming that one is willing to accept the consequences of one's "choices."

The whole notion of homosexuality as an "orientation" rather than a "preference" was also introduced by the homosexual community presumably to remove morality from the discussion of this phenomenon. After all, if this behavior is genetic, then gays simply cannot help being the way they are.

There is a growing body of scientific research in the area of human sexuality that is pointing to the conclusion that there may well be "a genetic/biological component" to homosexuality. One such scientist is Dr. Simon LeVay of San Diego's Salk Institute for Biological Studies, and I spoke at length in my first book on Dr. LeVay's studies. He focused on the hypothalamus that forms the floor of the third ventricle and is "the area of the brain that is known to help regulate male sexual behavior." LeVay examined four groupings of cells, "technically referred to as the interstitial nuclei of the anterior hypothalamus, or INAH.... Other researchers had already reported that INAH 2 and 3 were larger in men than in women. LeVay hypothesized that one or both of them might vary with sexual orientation as well" (*Time*, 9 September 1991, p. 60). Using tissue samples provided by routine autopsies of nineteen homosexual men, sixteen heterosexual men, all of whom had died of AIDS, and six women, one of whom had died of AIDS, LeVay "found that INAH-3 areas of most of the women and homosexual men were about the same size. In straight men this region was on average twice as large" (*Time*, 9 September 1991, p. 60). LeVay's conclusion was that there is, indeed, a biological component in homosexual behavior. Laura Allen, a neuroanatomist at the University of California, Los Angeles, maintains that the study is valid and that the conclusions "make sense."

The most surprising aspect of all this new, scientific research has been the reaction of the homosexual community. Professor J. Michael Bailey, an assistant professor of psychology at Northwestern University, who conducted research similar to LeVay's from a psychological point of view with similar results, was quoted in the 5 February 1992 issue of the *Chronicle* as saying, "I'm a little bit dismayed by some of the critical reaction in the gay community I get." Professor Bailey is being polite. The reaction of some in the gay community has been downright vicious.

When Dr. LeVay went on the "Donahue" show to discuss his study, he was brutally attacked by several gay guests. One was Dotson Rader, a gay freelance writer, who called LeVay's research "fascistic" and "homophobic." Another gay guest on the program who was very disturbed by LeVay's work was John DeCecco, a professor of psychology at San Francisco State University and editor of *The Journal of Homosexuality*.

Professor DeCecco maintained, "This [LeVay's] research has a political agenda. . . . He [LeVay] is making a political assertion about the causes of people's sexual preference based on his personal feelings, . . . but it's being couched in the language of science. It's not science." But, aside from his personal attacks on Dr. LeVay's motivations, DeCecco raised only one scientific objection when he claimed that there had been other such studies done before, and the people who conducted the studies were never able to replicate the results. LeVay said, "That's not true." LeVay was right. DeCecco was wrong.

LeVay's study was not the first to find a difference in the hypothalami of homosexual and heterosexual men. In 1990, a Dutch research team also discovered differences. In August of 1992, "UCLA researchers reported . . . that autopsies showed that the anterior commissure—a bundle of nerves that connects the left and right hemispheres of the brain—appears to be about a third larger in homosexuals than in heterosexuals" (*Time*, 17 August 1992, p. 51). According to Dr. James Weinrich, a Ph.D. in evolutionary biology and author of the book *Sexual Landscapes* who also appeared on the "Donahue" program with LeVay, maintained that a study done of twins concluded "that when one twin is gay, an identical sibling is three times as likely as a fraternal twin to be gay as well" (*Time*, 17 August 1992, p. 51). So, again, Professor DeCecco was wrong when he said that studies similar to LeVay's had been unable to replicate the results.

As I said earlier, there is a growing body of research strongly suggesting a biological/genetic factor in homosexual behavior, and the studies continue. In addition, as I reported in my first book on this subject, J. Michael Bailey, who is an assistant professor of psychology at Northwestern University and who I mentioned earlier in this chapter, and Richard C. Pillard, a professor of psychiatry at Boston University's medical school, also looked into the possibility of a genetic component in homosexuality, and the results of their research were published in the December 1991 issue of the *Archives of General Psychiatry*. According to the 18 December 1991 issue of the *Chronicle of Higher Education*, their findings "strongly indicate" that there is, indeed, a genetic component to homosexual behavior, in other words, reinforcing Dr. LeVay's conclusion from a psychiatric vantage point. Furthermore, Frederick L. Whitman, a professor of sociology at Arizona State University "says [another] twins study that he recently concluded but has not yet published came up with results similar to those of Mr. Bailey and Dr. Pillard" (*Chronicle*, 5 February 1992, p. A-7).

At one point in the "Donahue" program on which Dr. LeVay appeared, Mr. Donahue said to Mr. Rader, the gay freelance writer who called LeVay's research "fascistic" and "homophobic," "Your position is inhibiting inquiry."

Mr. Rader responded, "I *want* to inhibit inquiry because it [LeVay's work] is politically dangerous."

It is important to note that Simon LeVay is himself gay and that he was prompted into doing his research by the death of his lover of AIDS. Now, a rational, reasonable human being might be inclined to ask why this gay scientist is being branded with the epithet "homophobe" simply for approaching the question of the nature of homosexuality *scientifically*. As I suggested earlier, the homosexual community itself is deeply divided over the question of whether there is a genetic/biological component in homosexuality. While this may seem confusing at first, I suggest that the reason for this division is not difficult to figure out. It is because, as scientific studies continue into the nature of homosexuality, the politically correct positions of the gays and lesbians and those who presume to sympathize with their "plight" and cause become less and less tenable.

Let us, for example, address the question of homosexual behavior from the scientific vantage point of anatomy. There is no question that homosexual activity, especially in men, involves the use of parts of the human anatomy in ways in which they were clearly not intended. The tissues of the human anal tract, for instance, are clearly and naturally suited for expulsion, not for intake. Again, this is not a personal opinion or a political position; it is a scientific fact. That fact would explain the high and increasing rate of anal reconstructive surgery for gay men. So, again, while homosexual activity may be politically correct, it is anatomically incorrect. Because there is no scientific response to the point I just made, the PC crowd would simply call me a homophobe and *feel* as though both I and my point had been vanquished.

Undaunted by the vicious verbal attacks of the PC crowd, however, scientists have continued to press forward in their investigation of homosexual behavior, and so shall I. Let us, then, examine the subject from a naturalistic point of view. In other words, the question might be posed, "Is homosexual behavior natural or unnatural?"

If one is interested in addressing this question scientifically rather than politically, one must begin with Charles Darwin, the original naturalist. Now, Darwin informs us that the deepest instinct known to any species is the will to survive, and it does not take a Ph.D. in biology to know that this instinct manifests itself in the sex drive, which leads to procreation, which is how a species survives. In these terms, then, homosexuality violates the deepest, *natural* instinct of any animal, and a negative reaction to the whole concept of homosexuality, which the PC crowd calls "homophobia," may well not be learned through socialization but may well be nothing more than a "natural" response to something that we all know deep down threatens the very survival of the species. In other words, without heterosexual activity, the human race would cease to exist in a single generation. That is not a personal opinion or a political position; it is a biological fact, and calling someone who dares to point out that fact a "homophobe" does not adequately address the argument.

Given the politically incorrect, naturalistic/biological facts that the deepest instinct of any species is the will to survive and that without heterosexual activity the human race would cease to exist in a single generation, it becomes fairly clear that homosexual behavior is, indeed, not "natural," and the growing body of scientific evidence that is pointing to homosexuality as a genetic anomaly tends to reinforce that position. In other words, homosexual behavior may be the "orientation" of someone who is genetically inclined in that direction, but in naturalistic terms, one considers the whole species, and "normalcy" or "natural" tendencies are established by how most of the species behaves, and deviation from that norm is, by definition, abnormal.

Now some have attempted to answer the naturalistic/biological argument that homosexual behavior is not "natural" or "normal" by pointing to "homosexual-like activity" of other animals. For instance, one article points out that "cows frequently mount each other." While that may be true, when one examines the reason for this phenomenon, it becomes clear that such behavior is not what it at first appears to be. The same article quickly points out that "this [cows mounting each other] ensures that all the females coordinate their reproductive cycles and then produce their calves at the same time" (*Time*, 9 September 1991, p. 61). I assume lesbians are not trying to "coordinate their reproductive cycles" so that they can "produce their calves at the same time."

The same article points out that "female rhesus monkeys mount other females as a way of establishing a dominant rank in their troop's hierarchy." Again, I have never heard anyone speak of lesbian activity as a means of "establishing a dominant rank in their troop's hierarchy."

In a class I was teaching, a premed student spoke of male frogs "raping" other males. Again, based on the notion that many such examples of apparent "homosexual-like" behavior are very often not what they seem, I pressed the student for more information. The student finally admitted that male frogs did this because it rendered the victim impotent and left all the females for the assailant. The point is that there seems to be nothing in "nature" paralleling human homosexual behavior, which further supports the position that while homosexual tendencies may be the biological "orientation" of some, it is clearly a genetic anomaly and a deviation from "normal" behavior.

Finally, laboratory tests indicate fairly clearly that homosexual behavior is not the "natural" thing the PC crowd would have us believe. Roger Gorski, a neuroendocrinologist at the University of California, Los Angeles, "has learned that sex hormones (or the lack thereof) affect the anatomy of a rat's brain." By manipulating the testosterone levels of rats, Gorski "has been able to produce male rodents that demonstrate feminine behavior." He also "discovered a part of the brain that appears to be involved in regulating sexual behavior and is five times as large in males as in females. But without testosterone this specialized region shrinks in castrated subjects" (*Time*, 9 September 1991, p. 61). Now this, of course, suggests that homosexual behavior can be "treated" with hormone therapy, at least in rats, and I believe that this is what some in the gay community are so afraid of, and "homophobia," which we hear so much about these days, may be nothing more than homosexuals' projection of their own paranoia and deep-seated anxiety over who and what they are.

Yet another scientific question raised by all the research that suggests a genetic/biological component to homosexual activity involves bisexuals. If heterosexual behavior is biologically natural, and homosexuality is a behavior induced by a genetic anomaly, what accounts for bisexual behavior? In an article devoted entirely to bisexuality in the 17 August 1992 issue of *Time* magazine, the question is posed, "Are people essentially either straight or gay, with bisexuality being merely the unnatural by-product of confusion and repression among homosexuals?" John Craig, a writer who organizes weekend retreats for bisexual men, is quoted as saying, "I want to experience contact with a man's body and with a woman's body. That's just a basic part of who I am" (p. 50). The article also tells the story of Lani Kaahumanu, who is described as "a typical San Mateo, Calif. housewife, wed to her high school sweetheart for 11 years and the mother of two children." According to Kaahumanu, "the women's movement of the '70s" gave her the "freedom to love women, . . . She divorced and for four years lived what she calls a 'very public lesbian life.' But by 1980 Kaahumanu had fallen in love with a man" (p. 50).

In yet another *Time* article, June Reinisch, director of the Kinsey Institute for Research in Sex, Gender, and Reproduction at Indiana University, "cites the example of a woman who fell in love with and was married to a man for 10 years, then at the age of 30 fell in love with a woman and spent 11 years in that relationship, and at 41 fell in love with a man" (9 September 1991, p. 61).

In that same article, a person named only as Jason, a thirty-seven year old Seattle architect, claims, "We [he and his wife] talked about our marriage vows because I did not want to say 'I will forsake all others.' I couldn't vow monogamy." The article maintains that Jason "is faithful to his wife in one sense: his outside liaisons are limited to men, and only one at a time. 'Besides [Jason says], I can't handle too many emotional relationships at a time. You can get burned out' " (p. 51).

In my view, the only thing more ridiculous than Jason's statements is the seriousness with which mainstream media report these things. I submit that a rational, reasonable human being just might conclude that the most accurate word to describe the people just referred to is *confused*. This confusion is the result of the concerted efforts of the homosexual activists and their "sensitive" PC supporters to push their political agenda, an agenda that completely ignores all scientific study and assiduously avoids any discussion that could remotely be called scientific. As I have already demonstrated, the reason is quite simply that logical, scientific approaches to homosexual issues have divided the homosexual community. In order to maintain any semblance of unity, homosexual "leaders" must maintain a political focus. Their unspoken strategy is "Always talk politics, and call anyone who disputes any position we take a homophobe." Their motto could easily be "Logic Be Damned!", even in the area of AIDS, which is clearly the most disturbing aspect of the gay rights movement.

There is no area of the PC agenda where inconsistency and downright contradiction are more apparent than in the discussion of AIDS. First of all, we are told constantly that AIDS is *not* a "gay" disease, even though statistics from the Center For Disease Control clearly indicate that the *vast* majority of HIV-positive individuals are homosexual males. Even more compelling than the CDC's figures is an article that appeared in the 3 August 1992 issue of *Time* magazine. In this piece, Gary Kaupman, a journalist and AIDS activist, is quoted as saying that "AIDS has broken the playboy stereotype and exposed our humanity to the rest of the world, and that has allowed us to touch it better ourselves. We have been seen as more serious people, and we have become more serious people" (p. 35). Now this sounds like an admission that AIDS has had a profound and serious impact on the gay community that goes far beyond anything with which the "straight" community has had to deal. The article goes on to state, "AIDS has been the great defining moment in the history of the U.S. gay movement. By a macabre irony, the disease that wiped out so many gay men has given their survivors a sense of mature purpose" (p. 36). Again, that sounds strangely like a very special claim to AIDS by gays. The article continues, "The crisis [AIDS] turned an often hedonistic male sub-culture of bar hopping, promiscuity and abundant 'recreational' drugs—an endless party centered on the young and the restless—into a true community, rich in social services and political lobbies, in volunteerism and civic spirit" (p. 36). These and many other similar comments would seem to be a fairly clear indication that AIDS has disproportionately affected the so-called gay community, and specifically the gay *male* community. There were even complaints that lesbians have not been very sympathetic. Does this strike anyone as odd? Still, we are told constantly that if we perceive this to be predominantly a gay male disease that we are homophobes.

An even more troubling inconsistency is revealed in an article entitled "Invincible AIDS." This article, which also appeared in the 3 August 1992 issue of *Time*, states, "There is no vaccine, no cure and not even an indisputably effective treatment" (p. 30). The article goes on to state, "Despite dogged detective work by the world's best researchers, AIDS (acquired immunodeficiency syndrome) remains one of the most mysterious maladies ever to confront medical science. The more researchers learn about the disease, the more questions they have" (p. 30). It was also reported that at the Eighth International AIDS Conference in Amsterdam attended by over eleven thousand "scientists and other experts," "bewilderment reached a new level" (p. 31).

Now, I have said that this is precisely what is so frightening about AIDS, yet we have "education programs" all across the world that are giving out *definitive* information about this disease when the medical community has clearly said and continues to maintain that this is "one of the most mysterious maladies ever to confront medical science" and that "the more researchers learn about the disease, the more questions they have." Now, is it unreasonable of me to suggest that in the face of these facts that giving our kids condoms seems a bit absurd? Yet, "safe sex" and distribution of free condoms to teenagers remains the focus of most AIDS and/or sex "education" programs as well as of the commercials produced and being aired at taxpayers' expense at the behest of Surgeon General Jocelyn Elders.

Ms. Elders reaffirmed at a national news conference at which these commercials were aired what C. Everett Koop had stated, that abstinence is the best protection against HIV, the virus that causes AIDS. Yet, abstinence is never mentioned in the commercials! The closest the commercials come to advocating what is agreed to be the only foolproof way of avoiding contracting this disease is by having a panting young woman telling her panting young companion to "Forget it" when he tells her he didn't bring "it"—a condom. While the whole concept of "Just Say No" is constantly ridiculed by the PC crowd and their willing accomplices in the mainstream media and the entertainment industry as naive, we are asked to believe that two panting teenagers in the heat of passion can "just say no" and switch off their hormones as one would an electric light simply because they don't have a condom handy. I suggest that the contradiction is rather glaring to any rational, reasonable human being and that the logic upon which not only these commercials but our entire concept of AIDS education is based is not only inconsistent, it is, in the face of the "facts" about AIDS quoted earlier, absolutely terrifying.

Yet, the homosexual community, their "sensitive" allies in the PC crowd, and their willing accomplices in the mainstream media and the entertainment industry continue to push the notion that anyone who is concerned about AIDS is not really responding rationally and logically to a terminal disease for which "there is no vaccine, no cure and not even an indisputably effective treatment," but a homophobe. This kind of reasoning, which is rampant in the entertainment industry and in the dominant media, violates all categories of rational, logical thought. Need examples?

See the movie *Philadelphia* or the play which, according to *U.S. News & World Report*, is Broadway's "most anticipated play in decades [and] is a 3 1/2-hour apocalyptic epic about a fey former drag queen dying of AIDS." This Broadway hit, entitled *Angels in America* and subtitled *Gay Fantasia on National Themes*, is described as a "surreal, campy hilarious tragedy filled with such uncommon characters as a repressed Mormon Republican giving way to his homosexual yearnings . . . and an emaciated hero spotted with Kaposi's sarcoma." The play has already won awards in London and a Pulitzer Prize, and "before it had even opened in New York, it had sold $1 million worth of tickets." The article in *U.S. News* concludes with the claim that the play's apparent popularity "may be the most revealing poll yet of mainstream America's millennial mood" (10 May 1993, p. 20).

I would respectfully take issue with the article's conclusion about this revealing anything about "mainstream America." This play, and others like it, reveal only the "millennial mood" of the media and entertainment industry, which increasingly has as little to do with the *real* "mainstream America" as democracy does with the People's Republic of China. And, even though I have a Ph.D. in literature, I'm still trying to figure out what a "hilarious tragedy" would be. Sounds to me as though both the playwright and the critic are slightly confused. Nevertheless, the beat goes on as the "sensitive" sashay.

For an example of complicity in the dominant media, read David Gelman's piece on the fear of AIDS in the 29 November 1993 issue of *Newsweek* entitled "A Resistance to Reason." The piece is subtitled "Why do so many people—even some doctors—have an irrational fear of AIDS patients?" Please note how the word "irrational" always finds its way into the discussion of the fear of AIDS and those who are carriers of HIV. But, a rational, reasonable person might ask, what is "irrational" about being afraid of a disease that the scientific community has identified as "one of the most mysterious maladies ever to confront medical science" and that researchers have "more questions the more they learn about it?" Wouldn't the opposite reaction be the "irrational" one?

Nevertheless, Mr. Gelman also quotes two psychologists, Gregory Herek and Eric Glunt, who "found that many Americans are unconvinced by assurances from public-health officials that there is little likelihood of contracting the disease casually." Now, consider that statement for a moment. Exactly what are we being assured of? The fact there is "little likelihood of contracting the disease casually" means that it *can* be contracted casually. Right? And, if that frightens me and makes me want to avoid *any* contact with this disease, I'm a homophobe, right? And, how can "public health officials" give us any "assurances" when we are dealing with "one of the most mysterious maladies ever to confront medical science"?

Furthermore, wasn't it "public health officials" who saw no risk in exposing our citizens to radiation during nuclear tests and, therefore, didn't tell anybody that these tests were being conducted? Here is yet another example of the politically correct hypocrisy of the media. Anything "government sources" put out is treated cynically unless it deals with an item on the politically correct agenda such as "assurances" about AIDS. In other words, while constantly doing stories that leave the impression that our government can't be trusted, we are asked to accept unquestioningly their "assurances" about AIDS, and, if I'm skeptical about those "assurances," I'm a homophobe. Again, it would appear that logic and rational thought are on the side of fear and extreme caution.

Mr. Gelman also quoted Herek and Glunt as saying that "many discussants [in their sample] gave equal weight to all sources. Statements by a telephone caller to a radio talk show were assigned the same credibility as those made by a scientist or health official." Gelman concludes his piece with the sarcastic comment, "To get their message across, AIDS educators may have to phone it in." Mr. Gelman's snide comment would have the homosexual community and the PC crowd slapping their knees with raucous laughter because the jab is clearly directed at those "homophobes" who have "an irrational fear of AIDS." Yet, Liz Taylor's tearful plea for "global solidarity against a common enemy" at the Eighth International AIDS Conference in Amsterdam is reported with great solemnity. It strikes me that we are constantly asked to accept as very serious the "testimony" of movie stars and recording artists who probably never even went to college. Now, a reasonable, rational person might be inclined to ask, "Why should I care what Liz Taylor or any other Hollywood type thinks about a disease that is 'one of the most mysterious maladies ever to confront medical science'?" But, I suppose that my posing that question is just another symptom of my homophobia.

To make matters worse, the 3 August 1992 issue of *Time* also reported that "the AIDS epidemic is at least partly to blame for a new strain of tuberculosis that is extremely resistant to antibiotics. . . . Unlike AIDS, tuberculosis is highly contagious" (p. 28). It was also reported that "since the bacteria that cause TB is spread through the air, they threaten not only AIDS patients but healthy people as well" (p. 34). Now, a reasonable, rational person might be inclined to ask how a condom is supposed to protect one from this "new strain of tuberculosis that is extremely resistant to antibiotics" and "is highly contagious" and is "spread through the air." But, parents who might not want their kids in schools with HIV positive kids who just might also have this "new strain of tuberculosis" that is "highly contagious" and "is spread through the air" are just bigots. Again, while logic demands fear and extreme caution, the continuous PC diatribes about how those who are afraid of AIDS and all that is associated with it are just homophobes defy all categories of rational thought.

What is also so confusing is the incredible attention being paid to AIDS. On the list of diseases that are killing Americans today, AIDS just does not rank very high. The disproportionate attention being paid to this malady is testimony to the extraordinary power of the politically correct gay rights lobby. It also serves as evidence of the homosexual community's incredibly easy access to the mainstream media. But, could one not legitimately call the gay community's interest in AIDS "exaggerated"?

One might also be led to ask why the families of M.I.A.s from the Vietnam War are not allowed to have the same kind of impact on our national policy regarding the lifting of economic sanctions against Vietnam. The simple fact is that special interest groups with exaggerated concerns are allowed to be heard, but not to dictate policy, as was clearly demonstrated when Bill Clinton lifted the sanctions against Vietnam in spite of the protestations of the families of M.I.A.s. However, when it comes to AIDS, the community that is most affected by the disease enjoys disproportionate representation on presidential commissions and task forces which make recommendations that get quickly enacted as public policy.

The attempt to sidestep this obvious disparity would be to once again maintain that AIDS is not a "gay disease," that it, in fact, affects *everyone*, and *everyone* is at risk. Two logical questions then arise. The first, which I have already mentioned, is "If AIDS is *not* a 'gay disease,' why do the CDC statistics indicate that it is, and why does the gay community call it 'the great defining moment in the history of the U.S. gay movement'?" Second, "If AIDS *cannot* be contracted casually, as we are told, and most of us do not engage in any of the high-risk behaviors, how then can *everyone* be at risk?"

If this leaves you feeling as though you're drowning in a sea of contradictions, it's because anyone attempting to discuss the issues of gay rights and AIDS logically and rationally gets hit with a double-barreled shot of PC antilogic. As with all manifestations of the politically correct phenomenon, the focus is always on pushing the political agenda, and, like Hitler's Nazis or Stalin's Communists, it should not be surprising that their "logic" is not only full of inconsistencies, it often flies in the face of scientific and historical fact.

But, just what is the agenda of the politically correct, gay rights activists? What are their goals? The PC sympathizers and their willing accomplices in the mainstream media and the entertainment industry constantly tell us that "tolerance" is the main objective, but I suggest that their real goals go far beyond that. I maintained in my first book on this subject, have reiterated in interviews that I have done all across the country and in Canada, and reassert now that the real goals of the homosexual activists are the legalization of same-sex marriages, securing the same benefits for gay and lesbian couples that heterosexual couples have, the providing of adoption rights for such couples, and, through the educational system of this country, the teaching of our kids that homosexual behavior is normal and healthy and that if they (our kids) are not at least bisexual that there is something wrong with them, that they are somehow "not being permitted by their own and their parents' homophobia to experience the full range of their sexuality." I have actually heard an educator say this. Need proof?

In a piece in the 3 May 1993 issue of *U.S. News & World Report*, John Leo, in reference to the "notorious 'rainbow curriculum' controversy in New York City," said, "Instead of settling for a message of tolerance (gays are our neighbors and must not be harassed), gays and their allies inserted a passage saying that first-graders must be taught the 'positive aspects' of homosexual families. Another passage instructed teachers to include references to lesbians and gays in all curricular areas." Mr. Leo points out that "it is one thing to teach students not to harass gays. It is another to teach everybody that 'gay is good' as a way of improving homosexuals' feelings about themselves." But, there can be little question that the latter is being done in education. Mr. Leo also reported that

> in Massachusetts, Gov. William Weld appointed a commission on gay and lesbian youth that wants to go further than the rainbow curriculum. The commission's report calls for a broad array of gay themes and issues to be integrated into all subject areas and departments of all public schools. (p. 20)

Newsweek magazine also covered the developments in Massachusetts and reported that

> the governor's task force has recommended that schools [high schools and elementary schools] formulate specific policies to protect gay and lesbian students from harassment. The panel also urged special training for teachers and counselors, stocking school libraries with books and films for students who want to learn more about gay issues, and school-based support groups for gay students.

It was also reported in *Newsweek* that Rindge and Latin, an "elite" Massachusetts high school, now has a "Coming-Out Day . . . an autumnal rite every bit as gala as graduation day." Rindge and Latin joined Boston's Gay Pride parade two years ago, and the *Newsweek* story maintains that "at high schools around the country, multiculturalism has begun to embrace multisexualism." The article claims that "student gay organizations have cropped up in Chicago, Berkeley, Miami, Minneapolis, and New York. In Massachusetts alone, more than a hundred public and private schools have such groups." It is also maintained that "a climate of greater tolerance is making it possible for teens to explore more openly what they've historically sampled in secret. 'It's been going on for years and years, and now people have the courage to face it,' says Meredith Grossman, a Ft. Lauderdale, Fla. high-school junior." I have decided to simply quote the next section so as not to distort in any way what was said in this article.

> Some high schoolers are coming out homosexual, some bisexual. Others are admittedly confused. "It's very hard to figure out what you are in the core of your belly," says one Boston teenager who thought she was a lesbian until she found herself enjoying a relationship with a man. Teens' eagerness to experiment has made bisexuality almost "cool" in some schools. "From where I sit, it's definitely becoming more chic," says George Hohagen, 20, a Midwestern market researcher not long out of high school himself. "It's trendy to ask the question out loud: Do you think I am?" At meetings of Boston Area Gay and Lesbian Youth, support-group leader Troix Bettencourt, 19, a public-health intern, has seen an increase in teenagers who identify themselves as bisexual. They don't want to be penned into one type of behavior, he says. "It [saying you're bisexual] just says you're not yet defined and gives you some freedom."

... "They have gay assemblies, with speakers extolling the virtues of gayhood." ... At Newton (Mass.) North High School, students say that one female couple is constantly "making out" in the hallways and the cafeteria. ... According to Dr. Frances Stott, a professor of child development at Chicago's Erikson Institute, some adolescents may experiment because of a biological predisposition, some because they think it's the thing to do. But they also have a deeper agenda, she says. "Teenagers are at that point in life where so many aspects of their identity are coming together. They're figuring out issues of sexual identity, occupational identity, role identity. They're really asking the question, 'Who am I?'"

They're also taking cues from the popular culture. Psychologists say the media fascination with sexual athleticism and androgynous pop icons like Elton John, Mick Jagger and Madonna help promote experimentation among teenagers. (*Newsweek*, 8 November 1993, p. 68)

Again, I quoted this section at length so that no one could accuse me (the politically incorrect, white, heterosexual, Eurocentric homophobe that I am) of "distorting." I suggest the first question that a rational, reasonable person might ask after reading this is "How can school officials talk so sanctimoniously about 'self-fulfilling prophecies' when it comes to grouping kids according to their abilities and about the influence of violence on television and in video games and deny the influence all the emphasis being placed on homosexual issues has obviously had on our kids?" Once again, I suggest the contradiction is glaring, as they always tend to be with PC "logic."

As John Leo pointed out in his piece in *U.S. News & World Report*, the homosexual lobbies have thus far been fairly effective in keeping the debates "tightly focused on civil rights and homophobia. But not much attention has been paid to the phenomenon of homosexuality itself and the strong reservations about it held by people who are not bigots or haters" (3 May 1993, p. 20). I think Mr. Leo is absolutely correct. When one begins to discuss, logically, rationally, and scientifically, as I have attempted to do in this chapter, the nature of "the phenomenon of homosexuality itself," certain conclusions become inevitable.

As I have already pointed out, anatomically, homosexual activity is "incorrect" because it often, especially in the case of gay men, involves inserting "things" into body cavities that are clearly, physically designed for expulsion and not for intake. But, aside from being anatomically "incorrect," it can also be harmful and dangerous. Not only do the rising incidents of anal reconstructive surgery speak for themselves, given that the tissues of the anal tract rupture more easily than those of other body cavities that *are* physically suited for intake, the risk of transmitting and/or contracting HIV becomes higher.

Genetically, homosexuality is, at best, an anomaly rendering it biologically "incorrect." Given that the biological purpose of sex is procreation, one could even legitimately use stronger language. As Don Feder, a syndicated columnist for the *Boston Herald*, has pointed out, "Homosexuality is the metaphysical negation of life. Incapable of reproduction (giving life), it can replenish its numbers only by seduction." Such is the biological nature of the "phenomenon of homosexuality."

Philosophically, most of the world's great thinkers have concurred over the centuries that, in the hierarchy of desires, man's physical needs are the lowest, likening him to all other beasts. Often, man's physical desires can mitigate against those impulses that promote spiritual well-being. Even in the more ethereal Eastern mystical thought where the mind/body dichotomy is not a factor, self-denial leads to greater spiritual fulfillment. And since, homosexual activity can never fulfill the biological function of procreation, such activity cannot rise above the prurient. In other words, so-called platonic relationships based on altruistic *agape* exist on a higher level than those couched in self-indulgence, and, if one wishes to achieve "higher levels" of existence, one denies the self and the powerful prurient impulses. Thus would run the philosophical argument against indulging in homosexual behavior, even if such inclinations are genetic.

Please note, that morality has not even been discussed. From a moral point of view, the debate is even easier. When I was in graduate school, I took a course in world religions with a faculty member who was not only a Ph.D. but an ordained Episcopal priest. As we read and studied all the various Scriptures that are the bases of the world's dominant religions, I concentrated on finding areas of common ground, points at which the moral lines drawn by these diverse cultures crossed. When it comes to homosexuality, there is simply no moral ground upon which to stand. Virtually all Scriptures are specific and emphatic in their admonitions against such behavior. Yet, even with all the unequivocal condemnations of homosexuality by all the religions of the world, I am still willing to take the position that while I may judge behavior, I have no right to judge individuals. I can, in other words, hate the sin and love the sinner.

For the PC gay rights activists, however, the issue is not genetic or scientific or biological or anatomical or even philosophical or moral; it is political. Fine. My political position on homosexuality is based not only upon my moral judgment but also upon my profound and abiding respect for the Constitution, and it is quite simply this: What consenting adults do in the privacy of their own homes is between them and the good Lord and none of my business. However, when homosexuals take the most intimate details of their most private lives and demand that I view them in exactly the same way as they do or accept the label of "homophobe," I draw a hard, fast line. But, not only have homosexuals done just that, they have even gone further and, under the banner of "tolerance," are demanding special legal consideration based on their "sexual orientation."

A rational, reasonable person might be inclined to ask where all this "tolerance" will end. Nationally syndicated columnist William Raspberry hit squarely on the reason that homosexuals have attempted to keep "discussions tightly focused" rather than debating freely their real agenda and ultimate goals when he wrote, "Most of us are fair-minded . . . but suspect that something cultural is going on." Raspberry goes on to point out that there is a fundamental difference between a homosexual saying, "My sexual orientation and behavior are none of your business," and saying, "I demand that you acknowledge my sexual choices as the exact equivalent of yours." Raspberry also maintains that when the goal moves beyond tolerance and fairness "to embrace condonation of sexual behavior, a lot of people—not all of them bigots— start bailing out." John Leo also asserts "that a majority of Americans are simply unwilling to treat homosexuality as if it raises no moral or social questions" (*U.S. News & World Report*, 3 May 1993, p. 20).

Leo and Raspberry's positions are supported by polling information. *Newsweek* magazine did a poll 3–4 February 1994, partial results of which were printed in their 14 February 1994 issue. According to their findings, 65 percent of Americans say there should *not* be adoption rights for gay partners. Even Bill Clinton's pollster, Stan Greenberg admitted, "When the issue is discrimination, there is broad support, but when it gets into a type of marriage or family, the public is not very tolerant" (*Time*, 3 August 1992, p. 42). Perhaps that is why it was also reported in that same issue of *Time* that then candidate Bill Clinton "made it clear that [he] favors protecting gays under the Civil Rights Act, but [he] is quick to say that [he] does not support extending marital rights to gay couples." But, as John Leo points out, it gives rational, reasonable people "who are not bigots or haters" pause to think "that something cultural is going on," and that "the legal scaffolding for . . . attempts to establish same-sex marriages" may already be in place. Leo also maintains that "gay affirmative action and quotas" could also be hung on this "scaffolding."

Again, the question is, once we start "defining deviancy down" and rationalizing behavior that was once considered perverse rather than simply defending the rights of adults to act as they choose in the privacy of their own homes, how far will we go? Will we soon be discussing the rights of pedophiles? Now, before you dismiss me as a ranting, right-wing lunatic who jumps to extremes, consider this.

Newsweek magazine also did a story on John DeCecco, the professor of psychology at San Francisco State University who, as I mentioned earlier, attacked Dr. Simon LeVay on the "Donahue" show. According to *Newsweek*, DeCecco, who is editor of *The Journal of Homosexuality*, also "serves as an adviser to a Dutch magazine that advocates sex with children." *The Golden Gater*, the campus paper at San Francisco State, apparently "broke the story . . . that DeCecco sits on the editorial board of *Paidika, The Journal of Pedophilia*—a small, Amsterdam-based, avowedly pro-pedophilia magazine with a scholarly bent. DeCecco told *Newsweek* pedophilia is 'not intrinsically' wrong." DeCecco also reportedly asked *Newsweek*, "Are we going to let the sickos run society? Are we going to deny children, and adults, freedom to enjoy in life what could benefit them?" Want more proof that legalizing pedophilia is on the gay rights agenda?

On 22 February 1994, the *London Times* and Adam Rayfield of CBS News reported that the parliament of Great Britain had voted to lower the age of consent for homosexual sex from twenty-one to eighteen. Gay rights activists "booed" the vote as they originally demanded that the age be lowered to sixteen.

I think it is also important to note that in this country, the PC gay rights activists have taken a page from the playbook of the civil rights movement of the sixties. These activists are, apparently, intelligent enough to know that there is no way that politicians can safely embrace their radical, social agenda. Even when Bill Clinton "flirted" with that agenda when he pushed the gays-in-the-military issue to the front burner, he was finally forced to back off and came up with a "compromise" that the PC gay rights crowd is already challenging in court. So, it is in the courts where the gay rights activists have sought and continue to seek to achieve their radical social vision, avoiding the legislative arena. The legislative arena is much more subject to public opinion but ceases to be sympathetic when the "sheets are thrown back," so to speak, revealing the real agenda and ultimate goals of the politically correct gay rights activists.

Using the courts to implement their ideas of acceptable social policy is as far as the analogy between the PC gay rights movement and the civil rights movement of the sixties can legitimately be taken. Still, homosexuals speak of the two movements as though they were the exact same thing. I have been in situations where I have seen first-hand that this comparison infuriates blacks, who have, according to available polling data, a much stronger aversion to homosexuality than other ethnic groups.

Nevertheless, to understand the real agenda and ultimate goals of the PC gay rights crowd, one must follow the court battles for that is the theatre in which the war is being waged. Everything else, like the gays-in-the-military issue, is just a smokescreen. As I have said and continue to maintain, even if we give the politically correct homosexuals the benefit of the doubt and concede that they began by seeking "tolerance," they have certainly gone far beyond that now, and even though, as John Leo points out, "Gays have kept discussions tightly focused on civil rights and homophobia," the truth is starting to "trickle" out as court battles over same-sex marriages and same-sex couples' adoption rights continue to make the news and as people like John DeCecco continue to make statements (like pedophilia is "not intrinsically" wrong) that reveal just how far these people intend to push this business of gay rights.

But, there are some, like me, who refuse to play the PC game and allow "the discussion to remain tightly focused" when the PC gay rights agenda is clearly very broad with goals that are indeed far-reaching. There are many who, like me, are determined to discuss "the phenomenon of homosexuality itself" and to prove that "the strong reservations about it held by [most] people" are rational and reasonable and that the PC crowd's shrill cries of "homophobia" are, in many if not most cases, nothing but an exercise in *ad hominem* logic, which can legitimately be dismissed without a serious second thought. The bottom line is that "tolerance" and "acceptance" are two fundamentally different questions, and the PC crowd, with their typically intellectually dishonest tactics, is trying to confuse that basic issue. In my view, the only rational, reasonable position is: tolerance—of course; acceptance—*never!*

Chapter Seven

--------------------◇--------------------

Outcome-Based Education: Orwell's 1984 Plus Ten

I was a delegate-at-large to the 1988 Republican National Convention in New Orleans, and, being from Louisiana, I was also a member of the host delegation. Because I am also an educator, I was invited to and attended a seminar held in conjunction with the convention entitled "Excellence in Education." The seminar was sponsored by the McDonnell-Douglas Corp., and the panel of speakers included William J. Bennett, then Secretary of Education; Robert D. Orr, governor of Indiana; William Brock, former Secretary of Labor; and Terrel H. Bell, former Secretary of Education. I discussed this seminar in my first book on this subject, so I will not go into all those specifics again here. I mention it now simply to establish that I have had first-hand experience with the concept of "Excellence in Education."

The phrase was first used "officially" by former Secretary of Education Terrel Bell. It has been more than ten years since Secretary Bell convened the National Commission on Excellence in Education. This team of educators and public officials was charged with analyzing the state of public education and with making recommendations on how that system could be improved. The report they issued in 1983 was entitled "A Nation at Risk: The Imperative for Educational Reform." This report stated that "the educational foundations of our society are presently being eroded by a rising tide of mediocrity that threatens our very future as a nation and a people."

"The report cited more than a dozen 'indicators' to mark the decline of American schools" (*Chronicle of Higher Education*, 21 April 1993, p. A-19). Among other things, Secretary Bell's task force found "a virtually unbroken decline from 1963 to 1980" in scores on the Scholastic Aptitude Test (*The New American*, 23 August 1993, p. 1). Specifically, SAT scores "had plummeted more than 50 points on the verbal side" (*Chronicle*, p. A-19). The Commission placed the number of functionally illiterate adults at twenty-three million and found "about 13 percent of all 17-year-olds in the United States [could] be considered functionally illiterate" (*New American*, p. 2).

The report also indicated that

> scores on the Scholastic Aptitude Test had plummeted . . . more than 40 points in mathematics. High-school students in most states could graduate without setting foot in a laboratory or being asked to find a cosine. One in four mathematics courses at public four-year colleges involved remedial studies. (*Chronicle*, p. A-19)

The Commission further reported that "international comparisons of student achievement . . . reveal[ed] that on 19 academic tests American students were never first or second and . . . were last seven times" (*New American*, p. 2). I discuss these and other alarming statistics in greater detail in chapter 2 of my first book on this subject, so I will not do it again here.

Suffice it to say that, according to the *Chronicle of Higher Education*, the report issued in 1983 by Secretary Bell's National Commission on Excellence in Education "—bearing its ominous message of 'a rising tide of mediocrity' affecting American education—provided the bomb-shell needed to get people talking about the nation's schools" (21 April 1993, p. A-24). The Commission's report made recommendations for improving the educational system that amounted to a call for a return to the basics. The report urged the adoption of more stringent requirements in what it identified as "The Five New Basics," which included "English, mathematics, science, social studies, and computer science. It also called for more homework, a longer school day and school year, stricter discipline, tougher standards for teachers, more challenging curricula, and better textbooks" (*New American*, p. 2). The *Chronicle* also reported that the Commission's study and the resulting "school-reform movement . . . galvanized business and government leading to dozens of blue-ribbon panels, widespread state reforms—and a new generation of jargon" (21 April 1993, p. A-24).

However, the "Nation at Risk" report did not serve as a catalyst for the implementation of the "Back to Basics" reforms that were initially recommended by the Commission. On the contrary, the "widespread state reforms" that resulted as a response to the "Nation at Risk" report seem to have served to further entrench trends in education and further institutionalize "reforms" that were already well underway when the report was issued. What is particularly difficult to understand is that these so-called reforms seem to have been the cause of the problems in education in the first place. All these "reforms" have been gathered together under the new name of Outcome-Based Education (OBE), which is part of the "new generation of jargon." Speaking of jargon, it should be noted that OBE has operated under other pseudonyms, such as Outcome-Based Instruction, Outcomes-Driven Development Model, Performance-Based Curriculum, and Competency-Based Education. However, as the great poet wrote, "A rose by any other name . . ." But, just what is OBE?

According to Dr. William Spady, director of the International Center on Outcome-Based Restructuring and "widely acknowledged as the leading architect of OBE . . . ,

'OBE means focusing and organizing all of the school's programs and instructional efforts around clearly defined outcomes we want all students to demonstrate when they leave school" (*New American*, p. 3). While that may sound reasonable, it would behoove one to inquire as to just what the "outcomes" that "all students" will have "to demonstrate when they leave school" are. Here are some examples.

In Oklahoma, an "outcome" that students in grades nine through twelve will have "to demonstrate when they leave school" is this: "The student will develop communication skills, including being able to talk with one's actual or potential partner about sexual behavior" (*New American*, p. 5). Imagine that—a ninth grader talking to an "actual . . . partner about sexual behavior." Let's see—ninth grade—that would make these kids around fourteen years old, talking with "actual . . . partner[s] about sexual behavior." Isn't that nice.

One of the "outcomes" established in Oklahoma for a child in first grade is this: "The student will identify different types of family structures, so that no single type is seen as the only possible one." This "outcome," of course, could easily be construed as further evidence of the educational system's growing hostility to the traditional family unit. You will recall that in chapter 5, I discussed the positions of the politically correct gender feminists who view the traditional family, which "imposes the prevailing masculine and feminine character structures on the next generation . . . [and] enforces heterosexuality [which] is responsible for subjection of women," as "the cornerstone of women's oppression and would like to abolish the family altogether" (*New York Magazine*, 21 January 1991, p. 38). One would assume that among "the different types of family structures" that first graders in Oklahoma would "identify," families with single parents and families with same-sex parents would be included, and, of course, these children would be given no basis for making a judgment as to which "family" was preferable. I do not suppose that it would concern the compilers of

Oklahoma's "outcomes" that this approach ignores what *Cosmopolitan* magazine calls the "overwhelming evidence" that two parents staying married and raising their children together provides incalculable advantages, especially to the women and children of such situations. *Newsweek*, in its 30 August 1993 issue, posed the following questions:

> But does marriage really matter? Or is a family headed by a single mother just as good as the nuclear unit? The evidence comes down solidly on the side of marriage. By every measure—economic, social, educational—the statistics conclude that two parents living together are better than one. Children of single mothers are significantly more likely to live in poverty than children living with both parents. . . . Educationally, children in one-parent homes are at greater risk across the board—for learning problems, for being left back, for dropping out. (p. 21)

It would seem to a rational person that such information would be very important in an analysis of "the different types of family structures," but I seriously doubt that Oklahoma's OBE program, or any other for that matter, would include such statistics. As I have pointed out again and again, facts and statistics mean nothing to politically correct sophistic thinkers, unless those facts and statistics support their particular political point of view.

In Pennsylvania, the following "outcomes" are listed:

> All students make environmentally sound decisions in their personal and civic lives.

> All students develop interpersonal communication, decision making, coping and evaluation skills and apply them to personal, family, and community living.

> All students understand and appreciate their worth as unique and capable individuals, and exhibit self-esteem. (*New American*, p. 6)

"Roots and Wings," a national OBE program which will be discussed further later, lists the following as its desired "outcomes." "Children . . . will negotiate the future of the South American rain forest, manage an African Kingdom, write a new U.S. Constitution, sail with Darwin, and plan a transportation system for their own country" (*New American*, p. 6).

Now, even if one is impressed with all this, one still might be inclined to ask, where's the reading, writing, and arithmetic? The answer, unfortunately, is that those things are not there. In language arts instruction, for instance, phonics and grammar are replaced with a variety of "look-say" methods and "whole language" approaches, which seem as varied as there are teachers who profess to use such pedagogies. Furthermore, students no longer read from traditional lists of "Great Books." It appears that kids are often allowed to read just about anything they choose. Anthony Oettinger, a professor at Harvard, explains,

> The present 'traditional' concept of literacy has to do with the ability to read and write. . . . do we really have to have everybody literate—writing and reading in the traditional sense. . . . It is the traditional idea that says certain forms of communication, such as comic books, are "bad." But in the modern sense . . . they may not be all that bad. (*New American*, p. 4)

I would take serious issue with Professor Oettinger's use of the word *bad*. It is not necessarily a question of *bad* or *good*, but a question of quality. Are we to enable students by allowing them to believe that if they don't like something that that means that thing is not worth considering? I still operate under the assumption that teachers are supposed to assist students in developing a sense of taste for higher quality art. Would Professor Oettinger argue that there is no difference between appreciating comic books and understanding Shakespeare or Milton? I would argue that the difference is so significant that it becomes a difference not in degree but in kind. Alas, it seems that most of the advocates of these outcome-based approaches to education are more concerned with the fact that their students read and pay little or no attention to what they read.

What is even more important is that outcome-based educators do not seem to be concerned with whether or not students comprehend what they read. You can, for instance, have a situation where no two students in a class have read the same thing. One might ask just how a teacher is supposed to determine if the students have comprehended anything they have read since you can neither have a discussion of a text that not every student has read nor administer a test to the entire class if no one has read the same material. Sometimes, though not always, students are asked to keep a "reading log" in which they summarize what they have read, even though summarizing a piece of writing still does not necessarily demonstrate a clear understanding of the material. Sometimes, though not always, these summaries are checked by the teacher, but they are seldom if ever marked for grammatical errors because that, according to these educators, tends to intimidate the student and stifle creativity.

"Peer editing" is another "innovation" that is being used in language instruction. This involves the students "editing" each others' papers. One might be inclined to ask just how students are supposed to "edit" someone else's paper if they can't edit their own. When I have tried this in my own classes, I find that students will correct things that are not wrong and will miss glaring errors. While this, as well as some of the other approaches to language instruction, might have some merit, they can only serve a valid purpose if very closely supervised. Unfortunately, I know first-hand of a situation in which students were not only asked to "edit" each others' papers, they were asked to grade each others' papers. One student wrote on another's paper, "Your essay is racist," and gave the paper an F. What is even more astounding is that the teacher recorded and counted the grade.

OBE approaches also tend to stress "cooperative learning" over individual achievement, and many, if not all, assignments become group activities. I have used this method in my classes in the past. Inevitably, the "stronger" students, those who had been responsible about getting their work done and had good grades, ended up complaining to me that the "weaker" students, those who had not been keeping up and whose grades were lower, were not doing their share of the work. In other words, students who were inclined to "slack off" and just get by were being enabled by those situations because the more serious students were there to take up their "slack."

Furthermore, in outcome-based schemes, the traditional grades of K–12 are sometimes abandoned and children find themselves in "multi-age groupings." In addition:

> Traditional report cards with grades in individual subjects are abandoned in favor of check marks on a list of behaviors, attitudes, and skills.

> In high schools, the "Carnegie Units" required for graduation are abandoned. Instead of completing the traditional four units of English, three units each of math and science, two units of American history, etc., students are required to demonstrate ambiguous and subjective "learning outcomes" that cannot be objectively measured.

> . . . Community service is required for both children and parents.

> Training for 'global citizenship' is established as the primary purpose of education. (*New American*, p. 6)

These are just some highlights of the kinds of things that can be found in Outcome-Based Education programs, and it is not just the students who are affected. Teachers within these systems must earn and maintain teaching credentials. For the time being, this is done at the state level, but HR 6, the latest education legislation to hit the U.S. Congress with the National Education Association's stamp of approval on it, would have mandated nationalized certification for teachers. What all this amounts to, of course, is that control of schools is moving further and further away from the local level, which, in my view, is where it belongs.

Nevertheless, I think it would be helpful to get a historical perspective on the so-called school-reform movement to which the *Chronicle of Higher Education* refers. To do that, we must return to the beginning and follow the history of this movement, of which OBE is only the latest manifestation. The 23 August 1993 *New American* article on Outcome-Based Education contains much of the pertinent information, and, while I will draw heavily from it, that article does not present the information in chronological order, which I intend to do here. When I say that we should return to the "beginning," I refer to the point at which the "Nation at Risk" report indicated as the beginning of the decline in public education, i.e., the "early 1960s." I shall actually take it back a little further than that, to 1956.

I mentioned earlier several pseudonyms under which OBE has operated. There is at least one more OBE alias, and it is significant and instructive. Ann Herzer said, "Outcome-Based Education is essentially a more advanced version of Professor Benjamin Bloom's Mastery Learning" (*New American*, p. 3). Ms. Herzer is an Arizona school teacher and reading specialist who was trained in "Mastery Learning." Benjamin Bloom, a psychologist, published his *Taxonomy of Educational Objectives* in 1956, which "has become the epistemological and pedagogical bible" for the advocates of OBE. "Bloom's Taxonomy . . . was taught as holy writ in the educational psychology and teacher preparation classes . . . 20 years ago and is taught as same in most of the teachers colleges in the U.S. today . . . [and] forms the basis of virtually all OBE programs today" (*New American*, p. 7).

Bloom's study is basically an analysis of the human thought process or "thinking skills." His thesis is that thinking occurs in two domains, the "cognitive domain" and the "affective domain." The cognitive domain involves rational, concrete thought processes, and the affective domain concerns emotions, beliefs, and values. According to Bloom, cognitive thought processes are "lower order" levels of thinking. One moves from "lower" cognitive levels of thought (learning and comprehension) to "higher" levels of thinking (application and synthesis), the highest of which is "evaluation," which, according to Bloom, is "formulating subjective judgement as the end product resulting in personal values/opinions with no real right or wrong answer." The echoes of the ancient Sophists and the modern relativists are deafening in such a position. In another book Bloom wrote entitled *All Our Children Learning*, he took the position that "the purpose of education and schools is to change the thoughts, feelings and actions of students" (*New American*, p. 5). And so, as early as the late 1950s, a philosophy of education is advanced that posits the notion that the school system is an instrument of "change" and, *ipso facto*, teachers are the agents of "change." If Ann Herzer is correct, and I maintain that she is, it is upon this philosophy that OBE rests. But, let us continue the story and follow the development of this philosophy through the years.

Educational Leadership is the journal of the Association for Supervision and Curriculum Development, "a spin-off of the . . . National Education Association [NEA]." The *New American* article cites several very interesting quotations from articles published in *Educational Leadership* that clearly indicate that Bloom's call for "change" had been heard and internalized by educators. In December of 1964, an article appeared entitled "Leadership for Human Change." The author of that article, Harold G. Drummond, wrote, "The basic goal of education is change—human change. . . . We need to de-emphasize tradition and the past" (*New American*, p. 5).

Psychologist Carl Rogers published an article in the May 1967 issue of *Educational Leadership* in which he stated, "the goal of education must be to develop individuals who are open to change. . . . The goal of education must be to develop a society in which people can live more comfortably with change . . ." (*New American*, p. 5).

Also in 1967, the U.S. Office of Education (contract no. OEC-0-9-320424) published the Behavioral Teacher Education Project (B-STEP). "The primary goal of this influential program is stated as: '1. Development of a new kind of elementary school teacher who . . . engages in teaching as clinical practice . . . and functions as a responsible agent of social change" (*New American*, p. 5).

The National Education Association also set up the National Training Laboratory. "The NTL teachers manual says of children: 'Although they appear to behave appropriately and seem normal by most cultural standards, they may actually be in need of mental health care in order to help them change, adapt and conform to the planned society . . .'" (*New American*, p. 5). Concerned yet? Stay tuned.

In 1970, Professor John Goodland, former dean of the Graduate School of Education at the University of California at Los Angeles and currently director of the Center for Educational Renewal, wrote the "Report of the President's Commission on School Finance," a federally mandated and funded effort. In that report, Professor Goodland said that "most youth still hold the same values as their parents and if we don't resocialize, our system will decay. Parents and the general public must be reached. . . . Otherwise, children and youth enrolled in globally oriented programs may find themselves in conflict with values assumed in the home." (*New American*, p. 5).

In 1975, Dr. R. Gary Bridge of the Rand Corporation delivered a speech to a conference of educators. The conference was sponsored by the New York State Education Department. In that speech, Dr. Bridge also addressed the "problem" of students being too much influenced by their parents and "values assumed in the home." Dr. Bridge stated, "When the kids come to us at age four, five, or six, they already have these beliefs set. We have to unwind them and start over, and even then, we get them only a few hours a day" (*New American*, p. 5).

In 1977, the Chicago public school system announced that it was implementing a new program. The program was called Continuous Progress—Mastery Learning (CP-ML), and "it was hailed as 'a program that may be a pacesetter for the nation.' " Five years later in 1982, *Learning* magazine did a story on the results of the "pacesetter" program. It was reported that "a growing number of students, many teachers said, were entering high school having successfully completed the CP-ML program without ever having read a book and without being able to read one." More specifically, it was also reported that,

> Only 4 of 64 high schools scored above the 50th percentile, 34 [more than half] scored below the 20th percentile, and 5 schools, with a total enrollment of more than 7,500, scored at the 10th percentile (a score students could have achieved by simply answering the questions at random) (*New American*, p. 3).

At about the same time that Chicago embarked on its CP-ML experiment, the Washington, D.C. school system implemented a similar program. James T. Guines, Associate Superintendent of Schools for Washington and the chief designer of the program, was quoted in the 1 August 1977 issue of the *Washington Post* as saying, "the new curriculum is based on the work in behavioral psychology of Harvard University's B. F. Skinner" (*New American*, p. 3). It is interesting to note that Bloom's Mastery Learning theories have been called "pure Skinnerian, behaviorist, stimulus-response conditioning" (*New American*, p. 3).

B. F. Skinner, who worked mostly with animals initially, "developed teaching machines and even trained pigeons during World War II to pilot and detonate bombs and torpedoes" (*New American*, p. 3). Professor Skinner also "proposed that government institute a 'technology of behavior' to radically alter man and the environment," and is credited with saying that, "life, liberty, and the pursuit of happiness are outmoded and invalid goals that have no place in the 20th century" (*New American*, p. 3). Skinner also received substantial federal funding (seven million dollars from the National Science Foundation) for "developing and marketing his PACOS (People: A Course of Study) and MACOS (Man: A Course of Study) [which were] elementary school courses featuring promis-

cuity, cannibalism, murder, mayhem, adultery, extermina-
tion of the weak and elderly, and wife-swapping" (*New
American*, p. 4). Washington School Superintendent Guines
said, "If you can train a pigeon to fly up there and press
a button and set off a bomb, . . . we know that we can
modify human behavior. We're not scared of that. This is
the biggest thing that's happening in education today"
(*New American*, p. 4).

Unfortunately, Washington's experiment with its
school system had "the same tragic results" as the CP-ML
program in Chicago. In other words, while educators got
excited and continued their experimentation with innovative techniques and pedagogies all based on the notion of
"change," the kids' basic skills deteriorated. Yet, even in
the face of overwhelming statistical evidence clearly indi-
cating that these programs were abject failures whose
main victims were our children, the *Washington Post*,
quoting Thomas B. Sticht, Associate Director for Basic
Skills of the National Institute of Education, also reported
in August of 1977 that "similar techniques, called compe-
tency education or mastery teaching, are now being used
in many parts of the country" (*New American*, p. 3).

In January of 1980, there was a meeting of some forty
educators, and among them was Dr. William Spady. Dr.
Spady did an interview with *Educational Leadership* that
appeared in the December 1992–January 1993 issue. In
that interview, Spady conceded that "most of the people
who were there [the January 1980 meeting] . . . had a
strong background in Mastery Learning, since it was what
OBE was called at the time." And so, just in case there
were any questions as to the heritage of OBE, the definitive link between Outcome-Based Education and Bloom's
Mastery Learning is provided by none other than Dr.
William Spady, who, as I have already mentioned, is the
director of the International Center on Outcome-Based
Restructuring. Mr. Spady, "widely acknowledged as the
leading architect of OBE," said that the purpose of the
meeting in January of 1980 was "to form the Network for
Outcome-Based Schools." He also admitted that he

"pleaded with the group not to use the name 'mastery learning' in the network's new name" (*New American*, p. 3). Now, it is not difficult to figure out why Mr. Spady did not want OBE associated with Mastery Learning. It was obviously because of MLs dismal record in places like Chicago and Washington, D.C. What is difficult to figure out is why any intelligent person would want to continue applying a system of failed techniques and approaches and simply call it something else, in this case, Outcome-Based Education. But, that is exactly what has appeared to have happened. It would also appear that the word *obfuscation* and the phrase *intellectually dishonest* might well apply to Spady's effort to disguise the parentage of OBE.

Nevertheless, the next major development came in 1983 when Secretary of Education Terrel Bell convened his National Commission on Excellence in Education. As mentioned earlier in this chapter, this is the Commission that issued the "Nation at Risk" report, which found, among other things, "a virtually unbroken decline from 1963 to 1980" in SAT scores.

In 1984, G. Leland Burningham, Superintendent of Public Instruction for the state of Utah, sent a letter to Secretary Bell. Given the nature and direction of the quotations cited thus far, the year of that letter seems hauntingly appropriate. Nevertheless, in his letter to the Education Secretary dated 27 July 1984, Utah Superintendent Burningham wrote, "I am forwarding this letter to accompany the proposal which you recommended Bill Spady and I prepare in connection with Outcome-Based Education. This will make it possible to put outcome-based education in place, not only in Utah but in all schools of the nation" (*New American*, p. 7). This "proposal" Burningham and Spady, in conjunction with the Far West Laboratory for Educational Research and Development in San Francisco, submitted to Secretary Bell was entitled "Excellence in Instructional Delivery Systems: Research and Dissemination of Exemplary Outcome-Based Programs," and the program was launched with federal money.

In 1988, as I mentioned in the beginning of this chapter, the McDonnell-Douglas Corporation sponsored the Excellence in Education seminar in conjunction with the Republican National Convention in New Orleans. As a delegate-at-large to the convention and an educator, I was invited to attend this seminar. One of the things discussed at this seminar was the convening of an "Education Summit" with national education officers from the Department of Education, noted educational "experts," and, primarily, the nation's governors participating.

Also in 1988, of course, George Bush was elected president. According to the *New American*, "the big push for OBE on the national and global scale came with the election of George 'the Education President' Bush in 1988" (p. 7).

In 1989, President Bush called together all the nation's governors and noted educational experts for his "Education Summit." Bush's "Education Summit" produced the National Education Goals Panel, which articulated six National Education Goals. The "Education Summit" also mandated "federally contracted 'design teams' [which would be] involved in redesigning education." "Roots and Wings" and "The Modern Red Schoolhouse" are two of those "design teams." Consider the language drafted by "Roots and Wings" in articulating its goals and methodologies.

> [This program] will be one in which the school, parents, community agents and others work in a coordinated, comprehensive and relentless way from the birth of the child onward to see that children receive whatever they need to become competent, confident, and caring learners . . . no matter what it takes. (*New American*, p. 7)

If that language strikes you as rather dictatorial, consider this verbiage from "The Modern Red Schoolhouse." "Parents will consult with their child's teacher/advisor on a regular basis to follow and assist with the child's progress" (*New American*, p. 7). It does not sound as though parents have a choice as to whether or not they would follow these "recommendations." In fact, the *New American* article maintains that "parents will be drawn into the OBE web through mandatory 'parent training' classes and a 'Lifelong Learning' program that will require continuous retraining and recertification for every job" and that "under OBE, schools are scheduled for expansion not only to include day care, but to be merged with health, employment, and other social service agencies" (p. 2).

Also in 1989, Shirley McCune, senior director of the Mid-Continent Regional Educational Laboratory and an advocate of OBE, addressed the National Governors Conference in Wichita, Kansas. In her remarks, Ms. McCune said, "What we're into is the total restructuring of society. . . . You can't go into rural areas, you can't go into the churches, you can't go into government or into business and hide from the fact that what we are facing is the total restructuring of our society" (*New American*, p. 2). And so, once again, echoes of Bloom's notion of using the schools as agents of "change" are clearly heard.

Perhaps it is becoming clearer as to why some are concerned with the directions indicated in the totalitarian language being used by advocates of OBE, the disciples of Mastery Learning and the leaders in the so-called school-reform movement, language which has more than faint echoes of the social engineers of the nightmarish utopian society featured in Orwell's *1984*. Furthermore, this "reform movement" is not confined to the United States; it is global in scope.

On 5 March 1990, "representatives from more than 150 countries met in Jomtien, Thailand for a five-day World Conference on Education for All (WCEFA)" that was "sponsored by UNESCO, UNICEF, UNDP (United Nations Development Program), the World Bank, and other UN agencies" (*New American*, p. 7). Two documents were produced by that Conference, "The World Declaration on Education for All" and "The Framework for Action to Meet Basic Learning Needs." "The Framework sets forth six education goals, and they are almost identical to those set out by President Bush and the governors" at the 1989 "Education Summit" (*New American*, p. 7).

Back on the domestic front, in April of 1991, President Bush announced his America 2000 strategy for education. The introduction informs us that "the strategy anticipates major change in our public and private schools, change in every American community, change in every American home, change in our attitudes about learning." Sounds like a lot of "change." Mr. Bloom would, no doubt, be pleased. In short, implementing the America 2000 strategy would amount to nationalizing our educational system and, as I pointed out earlier, removing control of the schools from the local level. Toward that end, the Bush administration established the New American Schools Development Corporation (NASDC), which awards federal contracts to design teams like "The Modern Red Schoolhouse" and "Roots and Wings."

In May of 1992, Maxine Hairston, a professor of composition, published an article entitled "Diversity, Ideology, and Teaching Writing" that appeared in *College Composition and Communications*. In that article, Professor Hairston quotes several other professors of composition from around the country whose comments were published in major, scholarly journals dealing with rhetoric and composition. Although I quoted at length from Professor Hairston's article in chapter 1 of this book, I reiterate selective passages here as clear evidence that the mentality that schools should be used as instruments of social change and that teachers are the agents of that change—which was spawned by Bloom and Skinner and on which OBE is based—is alive and well among educators today. The professor who wrote the comments and the journal in which those comments were published are included in parentheses after each quotation.

> All teaching supposes ideology; there is simply no value-free pedagogy. For these reasons, my paradigm of composition is changing to one of critical literacy, a literacy of political consciousness and social action. (James Laditka in the *Journal of Advanced Composition*)

We must help our students . . . to engage in a rhetorical process that can collectively generate . . . knowledge and beliefs to displace the repressive ideologies an unjust social order would prescribe. . . . For instance . . . [the teacher] might openly state that this course aims to promote values of sexual equality and left-oriented labor relations and that this course will challenge students' values insofar as they conflict with these aims. (Patricia Bizzell in *College English*)

Teachers need to recognize that methodology alone will not ensure radical visions of the world. An appropriate course content is necessary as well. . . . the teacher must recognize that he or she must influence (perhaps manipulate is the more accurate word) students' values through charisma or power—he or she must accept the role as manipulator. (Charles Paine in *College English*)

Professor Hairston insists that "these quotations do not represent just a few instances that [she] ferreted out to suit her thesis; you will find similar sentiments if you leaf through only a few of the recent issues of *College English, Rhetoric Review, College Composition and Communication, Journal of Advanced Composition, Focuses* [all scholarly journals], and others." She goes on to say, "At least forty percent of the essays in The Right to Literacy, the proceedings of a 1988 conference sponsored by the Modern Language Association in Columbus, Ohio, echo such sentiments" (*College Composition and Communication* 43, May 1992, pp. 180–181). Assuming Professor Hairston is correct, and I maintain that she is, there is simply no rational basis for denying that the notion that schools should be used as instruments of "change" and teachers are the agents of "change," which was the original philosophical basis of the so-called school-reform movement of which OBE is only the latest manifestation, is the central focus of many educators' perception of the teaching profession today.

Furthermore, this "reform" movement with its emphasis on "change" does not seem to be slowing. It was candidate Bill Clinton, after all, who, during his 1992 bid for the presidency, challenged the American people to have "the courage to change," which, according to the education reformers, is what education is all about. It should also be noted that Mr. Clinton has praised the Bush administration's NASDC initiative, and he seems determined to carry forward on the education "reforms" initiated by his predecessor. Furthermore, on 31 March 1993, Mr. Clinton signed the Goals 2000 program into law, providing a new surge of federal funding.

As the chronology I have just delineated clearly indicates, the so-called school-reform movement did not begin in 1983 as a response to the "Nation at Risk" report. This "reform movement" has its philosophical roots in the late 50s and early 60s, and the pedagogies spawned by this philosophy, which have been in use for thirty years now, have within the last ten years been combined and codified into what has come to be called "Outcome-Based Education." In other words, what the 21 April 1993 *Chronicle of Higher Education* article refers to as "widespread state reforms" of education that came as a result of the 1983 "Nation at Risk" report appear to be not "reforms" at all but the further institutionalization of existing practices that began being implemented as "reforms" some twenty years earlier. In other words, as I pointed out in my first book on this subject, the so-called school-reform movement is not ten but thirty years old.

Even if one were to accept the position that the so-called school-reform movement began as a response to the "Nation at Risk" report and is, therefore, merely ten years old, we still must deal with the fact that there apparently have been sweeping Outcome-Based Educational "reforms" implemented since the 1983 "Nation at Risk" report was issued. It would seem rational, then, to consider what impact these reforms have had on our educational system. Unfortunately, all the statistical information we have indicates very clearly that the "erosion" of

American education described in the 1983 "Nation at Risk" report has continued.

In fact, the *Chronicle* article that is intended to serve as an update on this matter is entitled "10 Years Later, Many Educators See Little Progress for the 'Nation at Risk.'" Even former Secretary Bell himself admitted that "it [A Nation at Risk] hasn't left a legacy in that it has dramatically improved education" (*Chronicle*, 21 April 1993, p. A-24). Consider the following information.

In July of 1990, the Associated Press ran a story out of its Washington bureau that featured the results of a survey taken by the National Alliance of Business (NAB). The survey found that "64 percent of major U.S. companies are not happy with the reading, writing, and reasoning abilities of high-school graduates entering the work force" and that "72 percent of executives polled also thought new employees' math skills had worsened." NAB president William Kolberg, a former assistant Secretary of Labor and administrator of the Employment and Training Administration from 1973–1977, warned, "We are on a collision course with the reality that America is developing a second-class work force whose best feature compared with other nations will be low pay."

In August of 1990, the *Morning Advocate* (the main newspaper of Baton Rouge, Louisiana) reported that the College Board, a private, non-profit membership organization based in New York representing over twenty-seven hundred colleges, universities, secondary schools, and other educational associations, announced that scores on the SAT had dropped for the third consecutive year and that verbal scores had sunk to a ten-year low. College Board president Donald M. Stewart was quoted in that article as saying, "Reading is in danger of becoming a lost art among many American students—and that would be a national tragedy."

Then in September of 1991, an article published in the *Boston Herald* announced that verbal scores fell again in 1991 to a new twenty-year low. More specifically, "in 1972, 11.4 percent of the students who took the SAT scored over 600 on the verbal section. . . . In 1992, only 7.3 percent scored that high" (*Chronicle of Higher Education*, 3 February 1993, p. A-33).

I simply cannot resist a politically correct aside here. In the same *Chronicle* article in which the preceding statistics on SAT scores appeared, Charlene M. Sedgwick, a professor of English and director of the expository-writing program at the University of Virginia, maintained that "all the evidence [of deteriorating verbal skills] is anecdotal." Anecdotal! Now, this is a charge I have heard over and over again whenever I have talked about the politically correct virus. Virtually all the "evidence" of this epidemic is dismissed by the PC apologists as "anecdotal." First of all, just because evidence is anecdotal does not necessarily mean that it is invalid. Second, reducing an analysis of two decades of SAT scores to "anecdotal evidence" is amazing even for PC antilogic. Actually, Professor Sedgwick got her PC wires crossed. The typical PC response to such statistical evidence is, as I suggested earlier, to attack the tests themselves for being "culturally biased" or to dismiss the tests as irrelevant in terms of what they reveal.

Nevertheless, I shall now get to some legitimate anecdotal evidence all of which, unless otherwise indicated, appears on page A-34 of the same *Chronicle* article in which Professor Sedgwick was quoted. Edward W. Taylor, an English professor at Columbia, points out that "in the mid-1960s there were maybe 16 people teaching freshman English. Now around 70 TA's are teaching 2,000 students. In the intervening years, a program that was regarded as supplementary and remedial has become big business." Professor Taylor goes on to say that the reason for the burgeoning freshman comp business is that "there's been an overall decline; there's no doubt about it."

The *Chronicle* article also notes that "many professors at selective colleges and universities, even those who disagree that there has been a drop in overall writing ability, note some slippage in technical knowledge of grammar and sentence structure." "Slippage" is a nice euphemism.

I would use the phrase *appalling ignorance of "grammar and sentence structure"* to describe far too much of the student writing I read every semester.

As Sandra Pierson Prior, director of composition at Columbia, said, "That's a problem—when you want to write a short note on a student's paper saying that the verb doesn't agree with the pronoun, and he or she doesn't know what agreement is." I would suggest it's also a problem when one says that "the verb doesn't agree with the pronoun." A verb doesn't have to agree with a pronoun unless said pronoun is being used as the subject of the sentence in question. However, I will simply give my colleague at Columbia the benefit of the doubt and assume that that is what she meant, although it is difficult to see how we can demand precision and correctness from our students if we are not willing to apply the same standards to ourselves.

Nevertheless, Margaret O. Thickstun, director of the reading and writing center at Hamilton College, agrees that there has been a "slippage in technical knowledge of grammar and sentence structure" and says, "that many students don't realize that their papers need to be more polished" because "there has been a decision to emphasize creativity in many high schools."

Daniel J. Singal, a history professor at Hobart and William Smith Colleges, "has written at length about what he perceives to be a sharp drop in student preparation." Professor Singal also suggests that what has been going on in elementary and high schools is responsible for the "slippage." He said, "We see so many kids coming in with such weak command of language that even if we put in a tremendous amount of time it's not going to make a difference. Sometimes they are very motivated, but they are hindered by what happened in their previous 12 years of school." The images of kids reading comic books in English classes loom ominously in the distance.

Furthermore, many professors, myself included, maintain that the "slippage" has not just been in "technical knowledge of grammar and sentence structure." William

Rosenfeld, for instance, a professor of English at Hamilton College, says not only is he "absolutely certain that his students today don't write as well as their predecessors . . . the problems go down the line to punctuation and up the line to how to read a text, how to see where the heart of a paragraph is" (p. A-33).

George D. Gopen, professor of the practice of rhetoric and director of writing programs at Duke, also said, "Shallowness is a problem. The assumption that if they [the students] have an opinion it's right, or that if they give an example they have proved their argument—that's a problem." Professor Prior, director of Columbia's composition program, agrees and says, "Things are examined far less critically. When students challenge you, they speak from the gut or from anger and hostility. If you say, 'But what about this, or this?' they think you are not hearing them."

Professors Gopen and Prior have gone straight to the heart of the matter, the very root of the problem. But, as I pointed out in my first book on this subject and as I have reiterated in this one, the attitudes described by Gopen and Prior that are so widespread among students today are precisely the kind of thing to which relativistic, postmodern, poststructural, deconstructionist thinking inevitably leads. If one reduces truth and knowledge to mere matters of opinion and all opinions are equal, why shouldn't students challenge their teachers on virtually every matter that comes up? After all, the teacher's position is just his or her "opinion," and who is to say that that "opinion" is the correct one? Even my most liberal colleagues at the university are starting to complain that more and more kids come to us from high school who know a great deal about abortion and condoms and homosexuality but who can't read!

For more of what Professor Sedgwick called "anecdotal evidence" of declining verbal skills, ABC News recently reported that in 1993 the number of illiterate adults was estimated at over 90 million. That's roughly half of the adult population of this country and almost four times what it was when the "Nation at Risk" report was first released. When I heard ABC's report, the first question that came to mind was how many of those 90 million illiterate adults have high school diplomas. Nevertheless, if the 1983 "Nation at Risk" report can accurately be referred to as a "bombshell," as it was in the *Chronicle of Higher Education*, then ABC's statistic on illiteracy in America in 1993 would have to be dubbed a nuclear device. What that explosion and virtually all the statistical information at our disposal indicate is that whatever we have done in response to the 1983 "Nation at Risk" report has resulted in even further decline. In other words, whether the so-called school-reform movement is ten years old or thirty, it has not only *not* served to improve education in this country, it has actually made matters worse.

It must also be pointed out, as I did in my first book on this subject, that over this period of decline, spending on education has increased steadily from 2.8 percent of GNP in 1970 to 6.9 percent in 1991. In the 1990 to 1991 academic year, spending on education was a record $384 billion ($384,000,000,000.00), an increase of almost 7 percent over the previous year. Elementary and secondary schools enjoyed the largest increase, up 7.2 percent from the previous year to $231 billion ($231,000,000,000.00), and up 34 percent since 1980 to 1981. Per capita expenditures (dollars per student) in grades K through 12 rose 33 percent in the decade of the 1980s, and that is when budgets for social programs were supposedly being "slashed" by Ronald Reagan (another PC revision of historical fact). It should also be pointed out that these increases are after adjustments for inflation.

Even more disturbing is that the United States spends much more money on education in terms of total capital outlay as well as per capita than other countries that consistently outperform us in international competitions, as the "Nation at Risk" report indicated and as I discussed in greater detail in my first book on this subject. In other words, when it comes to problems in education, spending in this area is not a factor. It is not that we have not spent enough money on education. The problem is how that money has been spent.

I reiterate that while I am open to new suggestions and will support anything that actually does what it claims to do, the final word is this. The evidence is in on the "school-reform movement" and all its aliases, and it is time for a verdict. The evidence is clear, and the verdict is inescapable. Unless one is totally committed to playing games and ignoring overwhelming evidence, the inevitable conclusion is that it is past time to "unreform" education and return to approaches that produced measurable, positive results.

In chapter 6 of my first book on this subject, I enumerated and delineated five areas in which our schools needed reform, real reform. My proposals were very specific, and while I stand by them, I will not reiterate all those specifics here. Here, I will offer more general and philosophical conclusions and recommendations that, taken together with the reforms I suggested in my first book, would, I think, get us back on "the road to sanity."

We must resist any attempt to "nationalize" any part of our educational system. The evidence is in on the side of local control; the more local the control of schools, the less politicized the schools are and the more effective those schools are in producing measurable, positive results. We must also abandon the Orwellian notion that schools should be used as instruments of change and that teachers should act as agents of change. We must recommit our educational system to working toward developing our children's basic skills, which is the only legitimate role of an institution of learning and the only legitimate duty of a teacher. The extent to which educators play the role of "agents of change" is the extent to which we neglect our only legitimate duty, and I believe that we neglect that duty at the peril of our kids, and thus, the future.

Chapter Eight

———————◇———————

Christianity under Siege:
The Arena Revisited

You will recall that in chapter 5 of this book, I mentioned that Jan Schaberg, a professor of religious studies at the Catholic University of Detroit Mercy, wrote a book that was published by Harper & Row in 1987 entitled *The Illegitimacy of Jesus*. In her study, Professor Schaberg, a former nun (member of the Religious of the Sacred Heart), "contends that Jesus's mother Mary was not a virgin who was impregnated by the Holy Spirit" (*Chronicle of Higher Education*, 6 October 1993, p. A-7). Schaberg concludes instead that "Mary was raped." But, the "new scholarship" dealing with Christianity does not stop there.

You will also recall that in chapter 3 of this book, I discussed the fact that the "Great Books" of Western culture, the "canon" of Western literature, has come under increasing attack by politically correct scholars. Now, the Bible, specifically the New Testament, which is also one of the "Great Books" of Western literature, has also come under scrutiny and is a target for revision.

Robert Funk, head of the Jesus Seminar's Westar Institute in Sonoma, California, maintains that "the Christian movement hasn't seriously examined the question of canon since the 15th century. It's time for academic scholars to raise the issue" (*U.S. News & World Report*, 8 November 1993, p. 75). The discovery of the Dead Sea Scrolls and the so-called gnostic gospels, according to Funk, justifies this latest "examination" of the canon. Mr. Funk, sounding amazingly like a PC multiculturalist, also refers to the Bible as a "cultural artifact."

The Jesus Seminar, a "controversial panel of biblical scholars—which earlier concluded that Jesus spoke only a fraction of the words attributed to him—has begun a radical revision of the New Testament." This group, made up of "about 70 liberal scholars who since 1985 have been examining the historicity of the Gospels," met in the late fall of 1993 and "completed the first phase of a plan to redefine the New Testament canon" (*U.S. News*, p. 75). It is predicted that the Jesus Seminar "will likely recommend that at least some of the 27 books [which comprise the New Testament] be jettisoned and that other ancient texts be added." The Book of Revelation, which has been attacked in the past, will certainly receive particular attention and will likely be a target for "jettisoning," and "almost certain to be added by the scholars are such writings as the Gospel of Thomas, a first-century collection of Jesus's sayings found at Nag Hammadi [the gnostic gospels], and the Signs Gospel, a reconstructed text of what some scholars think is a lost account of the miracles of Jesus" (*U.S. News*, p. 75).

In her book *The Gnostic Gospels*, published by Random House in 1979, Professor Elaine Pagels, a religious historian, speaks of "self knowledge as knowledge of God." That, in fact, is the title of chapter 6 of her book. Professor Pagels also informs us that "many gnostics . . . would have agreed in principle . . . that 'theology is really anthropology. . . . For gnostics, exploring the *psyche* became explicitly what it is for many people today implicitly—a religious quest" (p. 123). That, of course, is not only a very "modern" concept, but also one that would hold much charm for a multiculturalist.

Not all the members of the Jesus Seminar, however, are in favor of the group's undertaking. Some referred to the undertaking as "presumptuous" and "argued that altering the canon is not an appropriate task for academicians." Stephen Patterson, professor of New Testament at the Eden Theological Seminary in St. Louis, said, "We are neither qualified nor commissioned to make these kinds of decisions" (*U.S. News*, p. 75). It is also sobering to recall that there was a "scholar" among the twelve apostles. It was Judas. Still, the effort goes on. In academia, it would, indeed, appear that nothing is sacred.

Philip Rieff, professor of sociology at the University of Pennsylvania, maintains that "the enormous perversity of modern culture and its academics is to teach the young that nothing matters and that the best attitude to have toward what came before is that of the most cynical of critics. Nothing from the past is worth anything at all" (*Insight*, 23 March 1992, p. 36). Although PC apologists would certainly take exception to the word "perversity," given the attitude that the proper role of education is "change," which goes all the way back to Benjamin Bloom and is being parroted today by advocates of "reform," and the notions embraced by "modern" thinking, one would be hard pressed to take serious issue with Professor Rieff's basic position. Referring specifically to religion, Mr. Rieff insists, "Students who arrive at universities rooted in a religious faith embedded by family, or who have a moral code they have adopted at their own choosing, are taught that the aim of education is to undermine these givens and show how inadequate they are" (*Insight*, p. 36). As an example of what Professor Rieff is talking about, consider the following "anecdote" that appeared in the November 1993 issue of *Campus Report*.

In the spring of 1993, a class called "English as Historiography" was offered at the University of North Carolina at Chapel Hill. The instructor's name was Barbara Ryan, a graduate student in English. Reportedly, Ms. Ryan began the class "by requiring all Christians to identify themselves," at which point she "told the class that in her experience, Christians were closed-minded, and lacking tolerance" (p. 1). According to the story, "Ryan's political agenda for the class focused on 'deconstruction.' She sought to 'deconstruct' the old-fashioned values her students had learned from their parents" (p. 1). As one might expect, the reading list for the course "was made up of works by minorities, feminists, and those of alternative sexuality, and radical politics" rather than "the traditional works and authors found in the typical course on American literature" (p. 1).

Catie McClure, a freshman at Chapel Hill and a student in Ryan's course, complained that "the entire course seemed to be a purposeful assault on my culture." McClure also said, "I was taught that virtually everything about America was worthless, that no intelligent person could possibly be religious, that clear standards of value in literature and life are an illusion, that everything I had been taught to love and admire could and should be 'deconstructed' " (p. 5).

According to the *Campus Report* story, McClure was "an 'A' student throughout high school and her first semester of college" (p. 1). The first paper she wrote for Ms. Ryan was "an essay celebrating family values" on which she received a "D." Ryan wrote comments on the paper which made reference to McClure's "unfamiliarity with this class's goals . . . and the need to figure out an overall agenda" (p. 1).

McClure's paper somehow ended up being reviewed by "a panel of professional writers and university professors who teach composition." The *Campus Report* story is not clear on just how this came about. Nevertheless, "none [of the members of the panel] felt that the paper deserved a 'D' grade. The consensus was that the paper was well above average" (p. 1).

The story goes on to say that McClure, "not willing to allow one feminist teaching assistant to ruin her academic record, . . . began to parrot back what the instructor demanded, criticizing American society and bourgeoisie values" (p. 5). When she did this, "her grades began to improve. By final exams, McClure got the ultimate accolade from Ryan, 'You're picking up on the class agenda very well' " (p. 5).

Several of Ryan's responses written on McClure's later papers were quoted in the story to prove "how willing the teacher was to reward the student's apparent ideological transformation" (p. 5). For instance, when McClure wrote, "It is especially challenging to reconstruct the appearance of women . . . because the current constructions are financially very empowering to investors of money in the American construction of 'beautiful,'" Ryan responded, "Yes, keep going. Have you read *The Beauty Myth*? It argues that women spending time on appearance give men a career advantage" (p. 5). When McClure wrote, "We may say that the way women have been constructed to look can be changed, but humans will always be constructed to believe and look certain ways," Ryan answered, "While we're straightening pantyhose and choosing exactly the right color blouse, they're negotiating business deals" (p. 5). McClure's closing remark, "we must attempt to examine the underlying conclusions in order to loosen ourselves from those which are most disempowering," drew this response from Ryan: "Good work—I'd frankly like to see more on how authors can make *change* [emphasis mine] happen, and how they can continually remind us not to accept any one norm as 'normal' " (p. 5).

There is really nothing more to say. Ms. Ryan's written comments are virtual summaries of the attitudes I have outlined in two books on this subject. These attitudes are very widespread in academia today, especially in the humanities. Furthermore, the fact that the grades of the student in question went up when she started to "give the teacher what she wanted" is the most serious indictment of all. But, Catie McClure's story is not an isolated "anecdote." I have read about and been told of scores of such stories that have happened all across the country. But, not all students are simply parroting back what they know their professors want to hear. Some students are actually internalizing the politically correct positions on Western civilization generally and Christianity specifically.

In chapter 4 of this book, I quoted from an article that appeared in the campus paper at my university. I reiterate selected passages from that article to demonstrate that Christianity is clearly under assault.

> Today, African-Americans are still faced with slavery—Mental Slavery. . . . The American system, which was created out of the racist ideology of Europeans, further developed the mental slavery among African-Americans and continues to do so today. . . .

> One of the key elements Europeans used to contribute to the slave mentalities of African-Americans was religion. Presently, European religion, "Christianity," remains the key element keeping African-American minds in bondage. . . . (*The Vermilion*, 8 November 1991)

Another article that appeared in the student paper on my campus was entitled "U.S. was not founded on Christian values." In the opening paragraph, the writer, Brian McCann, who writes a regular feature for the paper, claimed, "I was absentmindedly flipping through channels . . . , and for some reason, I came to a stop on this Christian fundamentalist show. The host, . . . like many hard-core conservatives, is usually good for a couple of laughs." You will notice, of course, the immediate lack of respect for anything traditional and/or religious, which Professor Rieff claims many academics regard as their primary responsibility to imbue into their students. Mr. McCann, of course, apparently knows his audience well. If you want a "couple of laughs" on campus, just make fun of Christians and/or conservatives. It doesn't even matter if what you say is accurate.

Nevertheless, Mr. McCann continues his diatribe by saying that "the host began spouting off that the United States was a nation founded on good Christian values by

God-fearing men." When the host warned "that the United States, like ancient Israel, surely would fail if we turned our backs on God," Mr. McCann claims that he "had heard enough." He demanded to know, "Just what did this guy mean by Christian values and God-fearing men? Nope. Sorry. I had to set the record straight." If you think that sounds arrogant, I should point out that Mr. McCann also said in his opening sentence that he "was just putting the finishing touches to a most enlightening column." I guess Mr. McCann doesn't realize that he cannot serve as the final judge on whether or not his own writing is "enlightening."

Nevertheless, in his effort to "set the record straight," Mr. McCann first points out that "of the original colonists who settled New England, only a minority were Puritans. The balance of the group consisted mainly of fortune hunters and the detritus [impressive word] of the English streets, poor houses and prisons." Mr. McCann also maintains that "more than half of the adult males in Boston by 1649 didn't belong to any recognized church, and in Connecticut only 15 percent of the adult male population joined the local church in the 1670s." He bases these assertions on a single source, one Richard Shenkman's book *I Love Paul Revere Whether He Rode Or Not*. Mr. McCann also insists that many of "the sober, stone-faced forefathers . . . spent their time consulting, or acting as astrologers, or maybe using what could be construed as witchcraft for protecting crops, divining the guilt or innocence of prisoners or just seeking out 'evil' witches." There are a variety of things wrong with this sentence. However, undaunted, Mr. McCann continues and asserts, "Benjamin Franklin never believed in the divinity of Christ, John Adams was fascinated with paganism, and Thomas Jefferson, Tom Paine and Alexander Hamilton subscribed to Deism." And, there you have it. American History 101, according to Brian McCann.

If Mr. McCann were my student and turned in such a piece of writing to me, I would suggest that he do three things. First, put a bridle on the ego, which seems to be running just beyond the boundaries of good taste. Second, and very importantly, I would recommend that he do a little more reading as the assertions made are, in some cases, half-truths and, in others, just plain wrong. Finally, I would inform him that he would have to dump the shallow, stereotypical thinking so evident in his comments. Only then could he hope to become a serious analyst rather than just another political hack. Toward that end, I would give Mr. McCann a quiz that would, at the same time, lead us in the direction of truly "setting the record straight." I would ask him to identify the source of the following "anecdotes" and quotations.

"Before the Revolution, the Anglican church in Georgia was supported by a tax, and under the first constitution, only Protestants were allowed to sit in the legislature." The last time I checked, I think the Anglican church was a Christian organization. Furthermore, "when the Bill of Rights took effect, five of the 13 states had government-sponsored churches, and most schools were church-run." Did you catch that, Mr. McCann? *Most schools were church-run!* In addition, "For literally centuries, until 1961, Maryland required officeholders to declare their belief in God." Last but not least, it was "in 1892 that the Supreme Court [of the United States] declared, 'This is a Christian nation.'" That was over *one hundred years ago!* Sounds like that "God-fearing" stuff and those "Christian values" really have been around for a good, long while, doesn't it?

And, can you guess where all these quotations come from? *Time* magazine, you know, that right-wing tabloid. In fact, the 9 December 1991 issue of *Time* also pointed out that a "1985 government-funded study of public school textbooks found that social-studies textbooks rarely mentioned religion at all, even when discussing events in which churches were a driving force, such as the abolition of slavery" (p. 65). That's right, Mr. McCann; churches "were a driving force [in] . . . the abolition of slavery"—that's Christian churches. Imagine that. *Time* also pointed out that that "government-funded study of public school textbooks found . . . [that] many books [also] omitted the deep religious motivation of Martin Luther King Jr." (p. 65). Remember him? He was a *reverend*, a *Christian* reverend. In fact, many of the leaders of the Civil Rights movement were. Jesse Jackson is a reverend, too.

Here are a few more tidbits from American history. See if you can identify who made the following statements.

"It is the duty of all nations to acknowledge the providence of Almighty God, to obey His will, to be grateful for His benefits, and to humbly implore His protection and favor." That was George Washington, in a proclamation he issued as one of his first acts as president of the United States.

"Almighty God has created the mind free—all attempts to influence it by temporal considerations are a departure from the plan of the Holy Author of our religion. I know but one code of morality for men whether acting singly or collectively." That was Thomas Jefferson, the one Mr. McCann said "subscribed to Deism."

Try this one.

"God who gave us life gave us liberty. Can the liberties of a nation be secure when we have removed a conviction that these liberties are the gift of God?" That was Thomas Jefferson, too! That little Deist Thomas.

Here's another.

"Indeed, I tremble for my country when I reflect that God is just and that His justice cannot sleep forever."

I know, I know, that sounds like one of those Christian fundamentalist preachers. In fact, that is *exactly* what that "Christian fundamentalist talk show host" was saying when Mr. McCann decided that he had "to set the record straight" and get "a couple of good laughs" in the process. Sorry, Mr. McCann. That was Jefferson again!

This one really ought to get you slapping your thigh. "Our ancestors established our system of government on morality and religious sentiment. . . . They believed that no government can be secure which is not supported by moral habits." That was Daniel Webster.

Okay, who said this?

We have been the recipients of the choicest bounties of heaven. We have been preserved these many years in peace and in prosperity. We have grown in numbers, in wealth, and in power as no other nation ever has. But we have forgotten God. We have forgotten the gracious hand which preserved us in peace and multiplied and strengthened us in war; and we have vainly imagined in the deceitfulness of our hearts, that all these blessings were produced by some superior wisdom and virtue of our own. Intoxicated with unbroken success, we have become too self-sufficient to feel the necessity of redeeming and preserving grace, and too proud to pray to the God that made us. It behooves us then to humble ourselves before the offended Power, to confess our national sins, and to pray for clemency and forgiveness.

Now that *has* to be one of those right-wing, conservative Christian types, right? Well, it was. As a matter of fact, the person who made that statement was a Republican, in fact, the grandfather of the GOP. His name was Abraham Lincoln. There sure does seem to be an awful lot of that "God-fearing" stuff in our heritage even though Mr. McCann informs us that the "U.S. was *not* . . . founded on good Christian values by God-fearing men," and he was "set[ting] the record straight."

One more. Who said this?

"It is the duty of nations, as well as of men, to own their dependence upon the overruling power of God and to recognize the sublime truth announced in the Holy Scriptures and proven by all history, that those nations only are blessed whose God is the Lord." Surely, you recognize old "honest Abe." That's right, that was Lincoln, too. Okay, Mr. McCann, I just can't resist giving you one more. Who said this?

"One day every valley shall be exalted and every hill and mountain shall be made low, the rough places will be made plain and the crooked places will be made straight, and the glory of the Lord shall be revealed, and all flesh shall see it together. This is our hope. This is the faith."

That was none other than Martin Luther King, Jr., in a little speech he gave entitled "I Have A Dream." Again, he was not only a Christian; he was a minister. In other words, Mr. McCann, if you really want "to set the record straight," read more than one book. Mr. Shenkman's *I Love Paul Revere Whether He Rode Or Not* is hardly the final word.

I don't mean to be too hard on Mr. McCann. I'm sure he's a good lad, and he is, after all, just spouting all the politically correct revisionist history that so many of my colleagues, people who really should know better, are imposing on students all across the country. And, the record really does need "to be set straight."

The plain, simple, sober fact is that the United States of America is deeply rooted in both Western civilization and the Judeo-Christian tradition. Those traditions moved and informed all our greatest leaders, the revolutionaries who gave us the Declaration of Independence and the Civil Rights movement. Anyone who denies that either is very uninformed or is being consciously deceptive. I do not presume to judge upon which this hostility to our religious heritage is based; I only know that it is so. I also know that, as with all other manifestations of the politically correct phenomenon, this hostility is no longer confined to the campuses.

In December of 1993, the *Wall Street Journal* reported the story of Beverly Schnell, "a 50-year-old divorced woman who works part time." It appears that Mrs. Schnell ran an ad in her local paper which read: "Apartment for rent, 1 bedroom, electric included, mature Christian handyman." She was then contacted by the Milwaukee Fair Housing Council and informed that "she had discriminated because her ad suggested that a 'handyman' or male was preferred. And 'Christian' implied that non-Christians wouldn't be welcome. . . . The Council offered to drop the case if Mrs. Schnell paid a $50 fine and $500 in attorney's fees." When she refused, the Council reportedly filed a complaint against Mrs. Schnell, and

in October [of 1993] the state of Wisconsin found

that [by running the aforementioned ad] she had engaged in sexual and religious discrimination . . . [and] the fines and fees would total $8,000. She fears she may have to take out a second mortgage on her house if she loses her appeal to the local circuit court.

The *Wall Street Journal* article concludes with, "We wonder where the limits are on the logic of this sort of litigation and administrative policing." Where are the limits? That is, indeed, the question.

At issue, of course, is the so-called separation of church and state doctrine implied, though never stated, in the First Amendment to the Constitution. However, if one is able to *read*, there is really no issue at all. The First Amendment states very specifically that "Congress shall make no law respecting an establishment of religion, or prohibiting the free exercise thereof." What's so difficult to understand?

The only kinds of people who can find an "issue" here are the most sophistic of deconstructionists, lawyers looking for cases to litigate, or people who are completely ignorant of the historical context in which the Constitution was written. When the framers of the Constitution prohibited Congress from the "establishment of religion," that's exactly what they meant, that there would be no hybrid Church of England in this country, a state church that citizens would be required to support with their taxes. To take such a simple, straightforward message and extrapolate it to mean that a non-sectarian prayer cannot be uttered at graduation ceremonies takes the most contorted and twisted logic conceivable, i.e., sophistic antilogic, but that kind of thinking now reigns in America.

Consider these select excerpts from an article entitled "America's Holy War" that appeared in the 9 December 1991 issue of *Time* magazine.

Last month the Pennsylvania Supreme Court threw out the sentence of a murderer who killed a 70-year-old woman with an ax, on the ground that the prosecutor had unlawfully cited biblical law to the jury in his summation urging the death penalty.

In Decatur, Ill., a primary-school teacher discovered the word God in a phonics textbook and ordered her class of seven-year-olds to strike it out, saying that it is against the law to mention God in a public school.

The town of Oak Park, Ill., blocked a private Catholic hospital from erecting a cross on its own smokestack because, councilors say, some local residents would be offended. (p. 61)

. . . *Lee v. Weisman* involves a Rhode Island rabbi whose bland prayer at a middle-school graduation was later ruled unconstitutional. The rabbi gave thanks to God for "the legacy of America, where diversity is celebrated and the rights of minorities are protected." The district court suggested that the invocation would have been fine if the rabbi had just left out all the references to God.

. . . California earlier this year ruled against the constitutionality of graduation prayers, as have Iowa and Rhode Island. (p. 62)

. . . "Angela Davis, a communist, was the speaker at my son's high school graduation," says Berkeley law professor Phillip Johnson. "People have to listen to the most heavy-handed dogmatism. Then suddenly the Constitution is violated if an agnostic hears the word god. This is absurd."

. . . Earlier this year [1993], a federal judge ruled that school officials in Wauconda, Ill., could stop a junior high school student, Megan Hedges, from distributing copies of an evangelical Christian newspaper, *Issues and Answers*. (p. 66)

. . . Dan Rodden, whose Caleb Campaign publishes *Issues and Answers* [says], "In the schools today there is definitely a religious and philosophical bent that is anti-Christian. Little children, by the time they're in second grade, know that God is illegal." (p. 66)

On 27 January 1838, in an address before the Young Men's Lyceum of Springfield, Illinois, Abraham Lincoln asked the ominous question, "At what point shall we expect the approach of danger?" His answer was "if it ever reach us, it must spring up from amongst us; it cannot come from abroad. If destruction be our lot, we must ourselves be its author and finisher. As a nation of freemen, we must live through all time, or die by suicide."

Today, America is a place where it is illegal to destroy the egg of an American bald eagle, but the government uses our tax dollars to destroy human embryos.

Today, America is a place where Marxists can burn an American flag in protest, but kids can't pledge allegiance to it in school.

Today, America is a place where you can't construct a crucifix on public property to celebrate Easter, but if you take that same crucifix and submerge it in a jar of urine, the government calls it art and uses our tax dollars to put it on display.

Clearly, something has gone wrong. One more time, I will ask you to identify the person who made the following statement.

"Public debt should be reduced. The arrogance of public officials must be curtailed. Assistance to foreign lands must be stopped or we shall bankrupt ourselves. The people should be forced to work and not depend on the government for subsistence." These observations were made in 60 B.C. by Cicero. By the way, were you aware that the historical designations of B.C. and A.D. are being abandoned so as to remove all references to God in historical dates? PC historians now use B.C.E. and A.C.E. (Before and After Common Era).

As I mentioned earlier, my learned colleagues dismiss my concern that Cicero's warnings have ominous relevance for us today with a smile and a shrug, and they say, "People have been predicting that the world was going to end for a long time, but it's still here."

"Yes," I say, "but the Roman Empire isn't."

Another anecdote that I think is illustrative is this. Three years ago, I sat on the Freshman Committee of the

English Department at my university. Among other things, we were responsible for selecting the textbooks that are used in the freshman courses. Because all students at the university must take these classes, the selections of texts are significant, if for no other reason than the sheer numbers of books that must be ordered. One of the texts we adopted, which I did not vote for, was entitled *Rereading America: Cultural Contexts for Critical Thinking and Writing*, published by Bedford Books of St. Martin's Press in Boston.

The text is divided into eight sections with several essays in each section. One of the sections is labeled "Harmony at Home: The Myth of the Model Family." The name of the section gives a pretty clear indication as to where this is going to go. As you might expect, one of the essays included in this section is entitled "The Gay Family" by Richard Goldstein, who "is the arts editor for the *Village Voice* [a newspaper published in New York with a reputation for being fairly radical] and writes frequently about sexual politics" (p. 477).

Mr. Goldstein's thesis is the familiar gay-rights argument that same-sex marriages should be granted legal status and that same-sex couples should enjoy the same rights and privileges that heterosexual couples do. As part of the "evidence" that Goldstein offers to support his thesis, he argues that there is historical precedent for doing this, i.e., legalizing gay and lesbian marriage. The example he uses is the Roman emperor, Nero, who, as Mr. Goldstein points out, "married two men, one of whom was accorded the status of an empress" (p. 481).

Now, is it just me, or is there a problem here? Mr. Goldstein has just used as the historical precedent to support his argument a figure who most serious historians agree was completely mad and who ruled Rome at a time when the empire was in an advanced state of decline. The questions that a reasonable, logical person might be tempted to ask are these: "Is this the vision Mr. Goldstein and the rest of the sophistic, antilogical, politically correct demagogues have for our culture and our nation? Do they, in fact, intend to lead this nation to the same place occupied by Rome under Nero? Is that *really* their agenda?"

The unfortunate answers to those questions are contained in Mr. Goldstein's essay. Goldstein has indicated, perhaps inadvertently but certainly clearly, that he apparently has no problem with America becoming what Rome was under Nero. It is just as unfortunate to realize that we are already well on our way to becoming just that.

I previewed some of the videos featured on MTV to decide whether or not I would allow my kids to order it for our cable. As I watched the "dancers," I kept expecting a black-hooded executioner to come onto the set holding the head of John the Baptist on a silver plate.

When the Pope visited this country last year, the one thing that he said that stuck with me most was "We must pray for America. She is in danger of losing her soul." Now, I will concede, in part, that the Pope's message was so poignant for me because I am a Roman Catholic. But, I do not think that is the only reason. I do not think that any thinking, rational person can observe what is going on in this country today and not be deeply concerned over the direction in which things are moving.

The other thing that struck me about the Pope's visit was the crowds that gathered to see him everywhere he went. Nobody packs a stadium like the Pope—no rock group, no entertainer, not even professional sports teams— and those stadiums were jammed with throngs of *young* people. What that said to me is that young people today are starved for *some* kind of spiritual guidance, guidance that they are just not getting from anywhere—in many cases not from their parents, in most cases not from their schools, and in some cases not even from their churches.

As I mentioned earlier, an analysis of the world's great empires when they were in their periods of decline is a sobering exercise. Such an analysis reveals that any culture, any people who either cannot or will not distinguish between acceptable and unacceptable, right and wrong, good and evil has one foot on the slippery slope of historical oblivion. While I do not believe that it is too late for America, I do believe that she has placed her foot on that slope. For her to remove it will take a spiritual rebirth in this country, which will only come if and when we rediscover the religious traditions and the God-fearing values that are our heritage. Only then can we hope to meet the challenge articulated by the ancient Greeks (also part of the Western tradition and, therefore, of our heritage) "to tame the savageness of man, and make gentle the ways of this world."

Here is one, final example of a leader who, in my view, understood the traditions upon which our country is based. I won't ask you to guess who this one was. It was President John Kennedy. The following is an excerpt from a speech that he was to have delivered on 22 November 1963 in Dallas, Texas. He never gave this speech, but perhaps in the silence of his death, his words might still speak to us today. He wrote:

> This is a time for courage and a time of challenge. Neither conformity nor complacency will do. . . . Let us stand together with renewed confidence in our cause, and the righteousness of that cause must always underlie our strength. For as was written long ago: "Except the Lord keep the city, the watchman waketh in vain."

> We in this country, in this generation are by destiny rather than by choice the watchmen on the walls of world freedom. We ask, therefore, that we may be worthy of our power and our responsibility, that we may exercise our strength with wisdom and with restraint, and that we may achieve in our time and for all time the ancient vision of "peace on earth, good will toward men."

More Good Books from Huntington House

Political Correctness:
The Cloning of the American Mind
by David Thibodaux, Ph.D.

The author, a professor of literature at the University of Southwestern Louisiana, confronts head on the movement that is now being called Political Correctness. Political correctness, says Thibodaux, "is an umbrella under which advocates of civil rights, gay and lesbian rights, feminism, and environmental causes have gathered." To incur the wrath of these groups, one only has to disagree with them on political, moral, or social issues. To express traditionally Western concepts in universities today can result in not only ostracism, but even suspension. (According to a recent "McNeil-Lehrer News Hour" report, one student was suspended for discussing the reality of the moral law with an avowed homosexual. He was reinstated only after he apologized.)

ISBN 1-56384-026-X $9.99

The Liberal Contradiction
by Dale A. Berryhill

Why are liberals who took part in student demonstrations in the 1960s now trying to stop Operation Rescue from using the very same tactics? Liberalism claims to advocate some definite moral positions: racism and sexism are wrong; tolerance is right; harming the environment is wrong; protecting it is right. But, contemporary liberalism is undermining its own moral foundation. It contends that its positions are morally right and the opposites are wrong, while at the same time, it denies that a moral law (right and wrong) exists. This is the **Liberal Contradiction** and it leads to many ludicrous (and laughable) inconsistencies.

ISBN 1-56384-055-3 $9.99

ORDER THESE HUNTINGTON HOUSE BOOKS!

_____	America: Awaiting the Verdict—Mike Fuselier	4.99 _____
_____	America Betrayed—Marlin Maddoux	6.99 _____
_____	Battle Plan: Equipping the Church for the 90s—Chris Stanton	7.99 _____
_____	The Burning of a Strange Fire—Barney Fuller	9.99 _____
_____	A Call to Manhood—David E. Long	9.99 _____
_____	Conservative, American & Jewish—Jacob Neusner	9.99 _____
_____	The Dark Side of Freemasonry—Ed Decker	9.99 _____
_____	Deadly Deception: Freemasonry—Tom McKenney	8.99 _____
_____	Don't Touch That Dial—Barbara Hattemer & Robert Showers	9.99/19.99 _____
_____	En Route to Global Occupation—Gary Kah	9.99 _____
_____	*Exposing the AIDS Scandal—Dr. Paul Cameron	7.99/2.99 _____
_____	The Extermination of Christianity—Paul Schenck	9.99 _____
_____	False Security—Jerry Parks	8.99 _____
_____	God's Rebels—Henry Lee Curry III	12.99/21.99 _____
_____	Gays & Guns—John Eidsmoe	7.99/14.99 _____
_____	Heresy Hunters—Jim Spencer	8.99 _____
_____	Hidden Dangers of the Rainbow—Constance Cumbey	9.99 _____
_____	Hitler and the New Age—Bob Rosio	9.99 _____
_____	Homeless in America—Jeremy Reynalds	9.99 _____
_____	How to Homeschool (Yes, You!)—Julia Toto	4.99 _____
_____	*Inside the New Age Nightmare—Randall Baer	9.99/2.99 _____
_____	A Jewish Conservative Looks at Pagan America—Don Feder	9.99/19.99 _____
_____	Kinsey, Sex and Fraud—Dr. Judith A. Reisman &	11.99
	Edward Eichel (Hard cover)	_____
_____	The Liberal Contradiction—Dale A. Berryhill	9.99 _____
_____	Loyal Opposition—John Eidsmoe	8.99 _____
_____	The Media Hates Conservatives—Dale A. Berryhill	9.99 _____
_____	Please Tell Me—Tom McKenney	9.99 _____
_____	Political Correctness—David Thibodaux	9.99 _____
_____	Prescription Death—Dr. Reed Bell & Frank York	9.99 _____
_____	*The Question of Freemasonry—Ed Decker	2.99 _____
_____	Real Men—Dr. Harold Voth	9.99 _____
_____	"Soft Porn" Plays Hardball—Dr. Judith A. Reisman	8.99/16.99 _____
_____	Subtle Serpent—Darylann Whitemarsh & Bill Reisman	9.99 _____
_____	Teens and Devil Worship—Charles Evans	8.99 _____
_____	*To Moroni With Love—Ed Decker	2.99 _____
_____	Trojan Horse—Brenda Scott & Samantha Smith	9.99 _____
_____	When the Wicked Seize a City—Chuck & Donna McIlhenny	9.99 _____
	with Frank York	
_____	Who Will Rule the Future?—Paul McGuire	8.99 _____
_____	You Hit Like a Girl—Elsa Houtz & William J. Ferkile	9.99 _____

*Available in Salt Series

Shipping & Handling _____

TOTAL _____

AVAILABLE AT BOOKSTORES EVERYWHERE or order direct from:
Huntington House Publishers•P.O. Box 53788•Lafayette, LA 70505
Send check/money order. For faster service use VISA/MASTERCARD
Call toll-free 1-800-749-4009.
Add: Freight and handling, $3.50 for the first book ordered, and $.50 for
each additional book up to 5 books.

Enclosed is $_____including postage.
VISA/MASTERCARD #_____ Exp. Date _____
Name_____ Phone: ( ) _____
Address_____
City, State, Zip_____

224